SHORT HISTORY

OF THE

34th BATTALION, A.I.F.

The Naval & Military Press Ltd

Published by
The Naval & Military Press Ltd
5 Riverside, Brambleside, Bellbrook
Industrial Estate, Uckfield, East Sussex,
TN22 1QQ England
Tel: +44 (0) 1825 749494
Fax: +44 (0) 1825 765701
www.naval-military-press.com
www.military-genealogy.com
www.militarymaproom.com

In reprinting in facsimile from the original, any imperfections are inevitably reproduced and the quality may fall short of modern type and cartographic standards.

FOREWORD

It is now forty years since the 34th Battalion, A.I.F., was formed and had the honour, together with other Forces of the Empire and our Allies, of halting and defeating ruthless aggression.

Over the ensuing years, dates, places and events have naturally somewhat faded in the memory of those who were privileged to play their part in that epoch-making period, but they still remember and will never forget the comradeship forged in the crucible of war.

Belatedly, this short History, written more or less in diary form, has been published with the object of reviving memories for that ever-diminishing number of ex-members who still remain, and who, when opportunity offers, congregate in order to keep alive the spirit of the Battalion.

Every care has been taken in the compilation, by reference to such Official Records as were available.

If there are errors, the Reader's indulgence is craved, in view of the years which have elapsed since the events took place. If some forgotten episode or name is recalled, then the effort spent in producing the book is fully repaid.

FORMATION AND TRAINING

The Battalion was formed in January, 1916, at the Albion Showground, West Maitland, from men who took part in the Wallaby March from the North West of New South Wales under Captain Cameron, Lieuts. Matthews and Moore.

Until 10th March, 1916, early training and formation of the Battalion was in progress. On that day the Battalion marched to the newly pitched Camp at Rutherford and was completed with the exception of the Transport. These joined later and came from the A.S.C. Camp near Sydney. Here strenuous training was carried out. The men were very keen and fit, whilst their comfort and health were made a special study. Food was good and ample and sports and recreation were not overlooked.

A Girls' League was formed to cater for the comforts of the Battalion, under the supervision of Miss Violet Mackay, who took a keen interest from the beginning, having, with the Mayor of Maitland, met the men of the Wallaby March at East Greta and prepared dinner for them on their arrival.

On 1st May, 1916, the Battalion left by train from Farley Station for the Showground, Sydney, equipped with kit bags and the necessary clothing, and was reviewed in Moore Park by General Ramoccotti. On the following morning, 2nd May, the men embarked on the Transport "HORORATA", A20, and sailed at 4 p.m.

The Battalion was under the Command of Lieut.-Col. M. St.J. Lamb. Major E. E. Martin, 2nd in Command. Lieut. C. E. M. Brodziak, Adjutant; Lieut. A. J. Gardiner, Quartermaster; Lieut. W. H. Salvatori, Transport Officer; Lieut. J. O. Smith.

The Company Officers were:—

"A" Company.—Major W. A. LeRoy Fry, O.C.; Lieut. R. J. Stewart, 2 I/C; Lieuts. J. W. Richardson, S. M. Harris, E. Shannon, W. W. Matthews.

"B" Company.—Captain H. L. Wheeler, O.C.; Lieut. T. G. Gilder, 2 I/C; Lieuts. H. Hicks, N. S. Cain, F. L. East, A. S. Whitlock.

"C" Company.—Captain J. A. McDowell, O.C.; Captain W. H. V. Baker, 2 I/C; Lieuts. H. H. Percy, C. S. Jeffries, G. W. Oliver, R. Wolstenholme.

"D" Company.—Major W. E. Foxall, O.C.; Lieut. E. Beaver, 2 I/C; Lieuts. H. S. Hill, G. T. Wood, H. C. L. Bennett, H. H. McMinn.

Captain G. R. C. Clarke, A.M.C.; Captain Chaplain A. S. McCook, Reg. Sgt. Major J. Garrety, Reg. Q.M.Sgt. F. Baulch, Coy. Sgt. Majors—"A" S. W. Barker, "B" L. Warner, "C" C. Finlay, "D" W. W. Edmonds; Transport, Sgt. T. Malone.

The voyage to England was without any unusual incidents and a good passage throughout. The first port of call was Albany, where three days were spent. Colombo was reached on Empire Day, 24th May. Here two days were taken up coaling and taking on provisions, etc. During the stay the Battalion carried out a route march through the town. Suez was reached on 8th June, where a party of Light Horse and some details were disembarked. Arriving at Port Said on 9th, the ship coaled and proceeded to Alexandria which was reached on 11th June, 1916. Here the Battalion transferred to S.S. "ARAGON", E867. Some Australian Details were on board, also a number of Tommies going to England on furlough. Devonport was reached on 23rd June, the Battalion disembarking at Plymouth at 1 p.m. and entrained during the afternoon for Amesbury, arriving at midnight and marched to hutments at No. 1 Camp, Larkhill.

Here the Battalion settled down to hard training, which included Route Marching, Trench Digging, Bomb Practice, Musketry and general Camp Routine.

Later the Battalion moved to No. 25 Camp and finished off their training, which included six days' battle practice and field work at the Bustard Trenches. Four days' disembarkation leave was given from 6th to 10th July and later King's Leave from November 5th to 9th. Whilst here the Official Colours were issued. Purple over Green (Oval), these replacing the Colours presented to the Battalion (Old Gold on Shoulder Straps) by the Ladies of West Maitland. A Signal Section was formed at Larkhill under Lieut. H. H. McMinn. The weather in England was mostly fine until the latter part of training, when a good deal of rain and snow caused inconvenience.

In October the Battalion was reviewed at a Divisional Parade by H.M. King George V at BULFORD.

The Battalion left Larkhill on 21st November and entrained at Amesbury for Southampton, embarking on the S.S. "ARUNDEL". The Transport left by S.S. "PRINCESS VICTORIA".

The allotment of Officers in France was as follows:—

C.O., Lt.-Col. M. St.J. Lamb; 2 I/C, Major E. E. Martin; Adjutant, Capt. C. Brodziak; Signal Officer, Lieut. H. H. McMinn; Medical Officer, Capt. G. R. C. Clarke; Chaplain, Capt. A. S. McCook; Quartermaster, Lieut. F. Baulch; Transport Officer, Lieut. W. H. Salvatori.

"A" Company.—Major W. A. LeRoy Fry, O.C.; Capt. R. J. Stewart, 2 I/C; Lieuts. J. W. Richardson, W. W. Matthews, A. W. MacDonald, C. O. Edwards, E. Shannon, T. Airey, T. C. Pittaway.

"B" Company.—Capt. H. L. Wheeler, O.C.; Capt. T. G. Gilder, 2 I/C; Lieuts. N. S. Cains, L. Warner, G. W. Oliver, J. O'Byrne, S. W. Barker, H. T. Hicks.

"C" Company.—Capt. J. A. McDowell, O.C.; Capt. H. H. Percy, 2 I/C; Lieuts. C. S. Jeffries, S. C. Finlay, B. G. Brodie, J. Waugh, A. J. Fell, A. E. Collings.

"D" Company.—Major W. E. Foxall, O.C.; Capt. E. Beaver, 2 I/C; Lieuts. E. St.C. Forbes, G. T. Wood, A. E. Watson, H. R. McLeod, H. C. L. Bennett, B. G. McKenzie, W. Edmonds.

Regt. Sgt.M. M. J. Garrety, Regt. Q.M.Sgt. H. H. Bevan, Coy. Sgt.M's. —"A" J. J. Cross, "B" J. A. Jennings, "C" F. Waugh, "D" A. L. Watson.

EARLY DAYS IN FRANCE AND BELGIUM

The Battalion arrived at Le Havre, France, on 22nd November, 1916. Disembarkation commenced at 8 a.m. and the Battalion marched to No. 1 Rest Camp on the Hill, arriving at 2 p.m. The men carried heavy loads, in some cases amounting to miniature Q.M.'s Stores. The march over the cobblestones was very tiring, notwithstanding the many route marches which had been carried out at Larkhill. However, after bathing their feet and receiving treatment, as well as partaking of a good meal, some spent a comfortable night.

The following morning the Battalion moved to Le Havre Railway Station, leaving "D" Company behind. On arrival at the Station entraining commenced at 8 a.m. and the train left at 11.15 a.m. The journey was slow and occupied until 4.30 p.m. on 24th. On arrival at Bailleul the men detrained and marched to Outtersteene. "D" Company arrived at 4 p.m. the following day. The Battalion rested here in Billets for two days previous to taking over garrison duties in the Line at Armentieres.

The C.O., Lieut.-Col. Lamb, with the Adjutant, Company Commanders, N.C.O's and Specialists went into the Line to inspect Trenches, Stores, Plans and to arrange for taking over this Section of the Line on the following day. The Specialists and N.C.O's remained in the Line. On 27th November the Battalion went into the Line in the L'Epinette Sector. The men were taken up by motor lorries as far as the Square near Houplines Station, and marched via Butterne Avenue and Willow Walk to the Line, carrying their packs and blankets into the Trenches. Lewis Gun ammunition was taken into the Line with the tin cases. The going was difficult owing to the condition of the Trenches and the heavy and bulky loads. Later the blankets were dumped near Tussage Dump, from which most of them disappeared. This was the main incident of our first relief in the Line.

The Sector taken over had been held by the Northumberland Fusiliers whom we relieved. Specialists of this Regiment remained for a couple of days to arrange and assist in the routine. We were greeted with a display of Verey Lights and, apparently anxious to see the newcomers, the enemy searched our Sector with his Searchlights throughout the night, which was misty and dark. Our Artillery and Trench Mortars put over a heavy barrage, either to let Fritz know we had arrived or to cover the change over; this was the signal for increased activity of enemy M.G. and Rifle fire to which the Battalion energetically replied. During the night Patrols were sent out, Listening Posts established and wiring was commenced. Dawn broke with thick mist hanging over the Sector and our men could get very little idea of the new frontage. Our Artillery and Trench Mortars were busy registering on enemy positions throughout the day and Fritz retaliated with M.G. and Rifle fire. The first day passed with no special incident. Our first casualty occurred on the following morning at sunrise when Pte Peck was sniped with an explosive bullet through the forehead. Counter battery work, M.G. firing and sniping were fairly active during our first term in the Line. Considerable damage was done to our Trenches and parapets and one of our Listening Posts was destroyed. Some enemy Patrols were dispersed by our snipers. Enemy working parties were fairly active on our front and his patrols were strong. Considerable road and rail transport was noticeable behind the enemy lines. The Battalion livened things up generally in the Sector which of late had been fairly quiet and Fritz did not appreciate the change. Just before being relieved we presented them with an issue of Gas. The Trenches were in a very wet and muddy condition. The water in the bottom of them being frequently frozen, the ice had to be broken to provide sufficient cover for the men, as the parapets were not high enough to allow walking on the ice. Thus the men had to stand in the freezing water and mud, with the result that the constant wet and cold caused many evacuations with trench feet.

The 33rd Battalion was on our left and the New Zealanders were on our other flank during this period.

After six days in the Line we were relieved and marched to Billets in Armentieres. The Battalion Headquarters were at No. 6 Rue de Strasburg, the Q.M.'s Store at No. 28. Billet routine from 4th to 10th December consisted of a general clean up and Bath Parades to Erquinghem.

On 11th December the Battalion went into the Line again, "B" Company occupying the Subsidiary Line instead of "D" Company, as in the first period. The weather was still cold and misty. The usual counter battery work was carried out by the Artillery and Trench Mortars. Some shells from our own "Heavies" dropped short and fell into our front Line. Sniping on both sides was again active. Extra Patrols were sent out to engage the strong fighting enemy Patrols in No Man's Land. The enemy was busy with his Working Parties and good work was also done by our wiring parties. Two extra Lewis Guns were added to the Front Line for the purpose of sweeping the enemy parapets and wire, in retaliation for enemy sniping which had become most active and was causing trouble. This was the beginning of continuous sweeping of parapets on both sides during the whole period of holding this Sector of the Line. Our Patrols were contesting No Man's Land, which up to this time Fritz considered belonged to him. Heavy bombardments were carried out which caused considerable damage to the Trenches and Supports on both sides. Quite a number of men were being evacuated with trench feet through standing in the cold and wet, notwithstanding that dry socks were issued every day to the troops. During this period there were a number of casualties, including 6 K.I.A. and Lieut. S. M. Harris, our first Officer wounded. Capt. W. Baker and Lieut. F. East and a number of men were also evacuated sick.

The Battalion was relieved on 18th December and marched to Billets in Armentieres. Capt. E. Beaver, injured by shell fire, and several other ranks, sick, were evacuated from here.

On 23rd December the Battalion moved to Reserve Billets at La Blanc Maison, where the building of hutments and stables for mules was carried out. The roads were flooded two or three feet deep and Carrying Parties and men erecting the hutments had to wade through this, in many cases waist deep. While here the C.O., Lieut.-Col. Lamb, left for Army School. Christmas Day, the first and what proved to be the worst in France, was spent in Billets, only in the course of erection. The Rations for Christmas Dinner were plentiful, but the cooking facilities were poor and the troops were somewhat "fed up" with the environment and bad weather. Each man had 1lb. of Pudding and a quart of Beer if he wished. The Pudding was supplied by the Comforts Fund and the Beer from the Regimental Funds. Working Parties had to be provided both on Christmas and New Year's Day.

On 31st December Lieut.-Col. Lamb returned to the Battalion and on 4th January, 1917, Headquarters and "A" Company moved to Jesus Farm and joined the remainder of the Battalion in hutments, which were now finished.

The following day Major W. LeRoy Fry left for the Training Battalion at Larkhill. A few men were evacuated sick and one, Pte A. Leach of the A.M.C. Staff, died.

On 24th January the Specialists went into the Line in the Houplines Sector. The following day the Battalion took over from the 36th Battalion, whose C.O., Lieut.-Col. Simpson, had been killed the previous day. On 29th January Major E. Martin temporarily transferred to command of that Battalion until 20th February when Lieut.-Col. J. A. Milne became C.O. The Front Line here was very similar to last Sector. During this period a good deal of shelling was carried out on both sides, the enemy sending over "Pineapples" freely. Aerial activity increased and many fights took place. Our Patrols were now gaining mastery of No Man's Land and Fritz was getting the "wind up". Verey Light displays, constant use of his Searchlights and the bombing of his own wire were common occurrences during the night time.

On 27th January Lieut. G. Wood, the first Officer K.I.A., was killed by shell fire. Also during this period the first N.C.O. killed in action was Sgt. W. J. Richmond.

The Battalion was relieved on 31st January and moved to Billets in Armentieres. Whilst here a number of men were evacuated suffering from trench feet and trench fever, caused by the appalling conditions in the Trenches, No Man's Land and Listening Posts. Working Parties were supplied, a general cleaning up carried out and Bath Parades held.

On 6th February Battalion relieved the 36th Battalion in the Houplines Sector. Patrols only occupied Listening Posts as the nights were very bright and moonlit. Our Trench Mortars put over a large quantity of shells, to which Fritz replied vigorously with "Minnies" and "Pineapples" but very little damage was done. Enemy planes were active over our Lines, but the Australian Aircraft drove them back. Air fights were frequent now. Also there was quite a lot of Anti-Aircraft firing, but no Planes were brought down.

Enemy Planes dropped bombs on our Sector and Working Parties, while his Working Parties were dispersed by our 18 Pounders. "Minnies" and "Pineapples" caused damage to our Trenches and our Artillery did likewise to the enemy emplacements. Lieuts. W. Salvatori, R. Wolstenholme and a number of men sick were evacuated here. The Battalion was relieved on 12th February and until 17th the usual routine of supplying Working Parties, general cleaning up, was carried out. The Battalion went into the Line again from 18th to 25th February and our Patrols were busy exploring No Man's Land. Enemy Patrols and Working Parties, which were strong, were dispersed by our Lewis Gunners. Snipers were very active and their Machine Gun fire greatly increased. From 25th February to 4th March the Battalion was in Billets and relieved the 36th Battalion on 5th March. Snow fell during this term in the Trenches. Enemy Planes came over our lines and dropped three white lights, which were followed soon after by a barrage of "Minnies". Our How's soon silenced them. Counter battery work was constant and the enemy dropped 14 H.E's into our Subsidiary Line as well as a very searching fire for our How's. The enemy Artillery became very active and did considerable damage to our Trenches.

From 13th to 17th March the Battalion was again in Billets. Lieut. H. Bennett was evacuated here. The Battalion occupied the Line from 17th to 25th March. The enemy persistently bombarded Hobb and Edmonds' Arc with 7.7's, 5.9's and 4.2's and had aerial observation throughout. Later quite a number of Gas Shells came over and a powerful enemy searchlight was constantly playing on Japan Road. On 17th/18th we released a quantity of Gas which brought retaliation of Machine Gun fire.

During the night of 19th March the enemy sent up red lights and our Artillery opened up in the vicinity of the S.O.S. Signal. Several craters and also gaps were made in the enemy wire. Our Patrols saw a large party leave the enemy trenches and advance to shell holes where they left bombs, etc., a number of which were connected by tape. The enemy had apparently been surprised when making a silent raid. On 20th Fritz put down a heavy bombardment on our Front Line, doing some damage. On the night of 20th/21st March, the enemy attempted a false S.O.S. by sending up Red lights, which was our S.O.S. Signal. Our Artillery opened up, narrowly missing one of our Patrols which was just about to go into No Man's Land. Having obtained the mastery of No Man's Land with our Fighting Patrols, Fritz apparently hoped to get our Artillery to open up on No Man's Land when our Patrols were out. However it did not succeed as a number of enemy dead were found by our Scouts, lying in No Man's Land. Owing to the snow-clad ground our Scouts were greatly hampered in their work. Fritz was holding Posts every twenty yards on our Front, which were strongly manned, and was very active digging communication Trenches.

From 25th March until 2nd April the Battalion was in Billets at Armentieres. Capt. C. Brodziak left the Battalion for England and Major H. Wheeler took over the position of Adjutant. Major W. Foxall, Lieuts. H. Hicks, H. McLeod and 32 O/R's were evacuated sick. Lieuts. J. W. Richardson and A. Whitlock were appointed Captains.

The Battalion again occupied the Trenches from 2nd April to 9th April. The snow was still on the ground and greatly hampered movements. There was normal Artillery and Aerial activity on both sides, with the Anti-Aircraft busy. The enemy was showing signs of attack during this period, but nothing came of it. Lieut. A. J. Fell was evacuated here.

On being relieved by the 40th Battalion, the Battalion returned to Billets at Armentieres. This concluded the early period of holding the Trenches and Line. The weather had been most severe. The worst winter France had experienced for many years.

First there had been continuous heavy rain, causing the men to stand almost knee deep in mud and water for hours, whilst holding the Bays. The Patrols and Scouts having to crawl over mud and shell churned ground in No Man's Land. Wiring and Working Parties had many hard and unpleasant tasks. Trenches were continually being blown in and had to be repaired. The men suffered badly from Trench Feet and Fever although dry socks were issued daily. During the rest periods in Billets however the men made the best of things while they could.

BILLET ROUTINE

When the period for relief is due, an Officer and N.C.O's from each Company, as Billeting Party, move out to the area and arrange Billets. Quite often not an easy matter to fix up. On coming out of the Line men are conducted by their N.C.O. Guides to their respective quarters. This is generally carried out during the hours of darkness. Coy. Q.M.Sgts. make arrangements for a hot meal on their arrival and the drawing of Blankets. Mail and parcels are the first things sought after. Baths are provided. Clean clothes and, where necessary, equipment are issued. Followed by a reorganisation of Platoons and a general cleaning up of equipment, etc.

Pay Day is generally a day or two after arriving at the Billets. The Regimental Canteen and Y.M.C.A. are well patronised for Smoking Requisites, Writing Pads, Tinned Fruits, Toilet Requisites, Chocolates and other luxuries which are in great demand for a few days. Ways and means are found to play the National Game of "TWO UP" and the Estaminets are not forgotten. Eggs and Chips are freely sought when it is possible to secure them. Sports and Games are organised and the best use made of time not taken up by parades and training generally.

DEFENCE OF ARMENTIERES

The duty of the Battalion is to supply Troops for the Firing Line, Support Line and Subsidiary Lines. Patrols for No Man's Land, Sentry Groups, Bombing Parties, Lewis Gun Teams, Gas Guards, and Wiring Parties. Also Working Parties to repair Trenches, build Dugouts, Ammunition and Ration Carriers, Stretcher Bearers and to carry out general routine work in accordance with the Defence Scheme laid out for each particular Sector.

GENERAL DESCRIPTION OF DEFENCE SCHEME

THE FRONT LINE is continuous but is organised into a series of defended localities. Between these localities are gaps which are not garrisoned but are patrolled by night. At night a certain amount of sniping and Lewis Gun fire is carried out from these gaps, in order to give them the appearance of being held. Medium and Light Trench Mortars also fire from these gaps to avoid drawing retaliation fire into the localities. The gaps are under enfilade fire from the flanks of each locality. The parados are demolished and dummies erected with barb wire and canvas sheets, so that the enemy cannot consolidate the position if he enters the gaps.

THE SUBSIDIARY LINE is organised in a series of defended localities with supplies of water and ammunition stores in them. When troops are sent forward from the Subsidiary Line to counter attack or for the purpose of reinforcing the Front Line, a sufficient number of men will be left in the Subsidiary to hold it according to the tactical situation, until support or reinforcements arrive under Brigade arrangements. To ensure this C.O's of Subsectors must maintain constant touch with Brigade Headquarters.

SYSTEM OF HOLDING THE FRONT LINE.—To economise troops and reduce casualties, the Front Line is held as thinly as possible consistent with safety. The general principle, on which all action in case of attack is based, is that no body of troops to whom portion of the defence Line or a defended locality is allotted, will give it up under any circumstances. If a portion of the Line is lost the troops on the flanks will not fall back, but will counter attack at once by bombing from the flank.

All Officers realise that the difficulties of delivering a successful counter attack are increased enormously if the enemy is given time to consolidate his position. Counter attacks will therefore be delivered at the earliest possible moment.

DEFENCE RESPONSIBILIY.—The general principle is that troops who are in occupation of the Line of Defence, position or system are responsible for providing nucleus garrisons for the next Line in rear until these are relieved. Battalions on the right and left flanks of Subsectors are primarily responsible for the occupation and defence of the Front Line system.

ACTION UNDER SPECIAL CIRCUMSTANCES.—In the event of the Brigade on either flank being compelled to fall back through enemy attack, Centre Battalion will act in accordance with instructions previously issued for such emergency. Prompt action in all cases will be necessary.

GAS ATTACK.—Special orders have been issued in the event of a Gas Attack for the Town of Armentieres. Sirens and Strombos Horns and the ringing of Church Bells will give the necessary warning. The Signal Company being responsible for warning when reports come in from the Sector where Gas is reported.

RELIEF.—Reliefs to be carried out every six days or as near to this as circumstances permit. Such reliefs to be carried out under cover of darkness.

TRENCH STORES consist of Small Arms Ammunition, Bombs, Grenades, Reserve Ration and Water Dumps, Engineer Stores, Picks, Shovels, Wire, A Frames, Duck Boards, Sandbags, Gum Boots, Food Containers, Gas Alarms, Periscopes, Trench Stretchers and French Maps.

LINES OF COMMUNICATION are established between Battalion Headquarters and Company Headquarters by Telephone, Visual, Pigeon, Power Buzzer and Runners.

First Line Transport is situated as near the Quartermaster's Store as is consistent with safety. Rations, Water, Ammunition, Engineer Stores are taken up daily either by Limbers or Motor Lorry to Dumps, thence by Carrying Parties to where required.

On 11th April the Battalion moved to St. Omer and entrained for Bayenghem-lez-Seninghem to train for the Messines operation, from 13th to 24th April. Lieut. E. Forbes was evacuated. Just prior to the Battalion leaving for Bayenghem-lez-Seninghem, Lieut.-Col. M. Lamb left for duty with the 9th Training Battalion. Major E. E. Martin took over command of the Battalion with the rank of Temporary Lieut.-Colonel. Lieut.-Col. Lamb when addressing the earlier reinforcements for the Battalion, caused some amusement amongst the men by his usual remark, "Stand back, you old warriors; I want to address the new men".

Having finished the strenuous training period at Bayenghem-lez-Seninghem, on 25th April the Battalion marched from there via Arques to Renescure. The next day the march continued to Pt Sec Bois and the following day to Armentieres, where the Battalion arrived at 3 p.m. very tired and went into Billets at Ecole Proffesionole. Here the 4th Reinforcements joined the Battalion. The men were employed on Working Parties until 3rd May, when a move was made to Billets at Le Bizet. Working Parties were supplied for the Front Line for the building of Breastworks, digging Trenches and carrying for the Engineers working at the Dumps. Whilst in these Billets the enemy shelled heavily, doing damage to the Billets and causing a few casualties. The Roads, Dumps and Working Parties were constantly under heavy enemy fire.

On the night of 6th May the Billets were heavily shelled at 9.30 p.m., 10.30 p.m. and 2.30 a.m. One 4.2 shell fell in the Officers' Mess Room. 300 Rounds were fired in and around the Billets and every one had a very unpleasant time generally.

The following day two Companies moved to the Subsidiary Line and two went to Pont de Nieppe. No troops remaining in Le Bizet after 8.30 p.m. At that hour every Gun and Howitzer, except 12-inch, in the Second Army fired for five minutes at intense rate and again at 11 p.m. The Barrage presented a beautiful sight and was done with the object of checking the enemy shelling the back areas.

On 8th May the Battalion became "B" Battalion and went into reserve at Le Touquet as follows:—"A" Coy.—2 Platoons at "Lys Farm", 2 Platoons at "Tancred Farm". "B" Coy.—2 Platoons at "Gunners Farm", 2 Platoons at "Grand Rateque". "C" Coy.—2 Platoons at "Maison 1875 N", 1 Platoon at "Maison 1875 S". "D" Coy at "Delville Farm" with 1 support Platoon at "Support Farm". The enemy sent over 310 rounds of "5.9's" and "4.2's" in two hours, but there were no casualties. The back areas were getting a lively time from enemy fire. Battalion Headquarters moved from "Neill de Rose" to "Gendarme". Whilst holding these Strong Posts an enemy Plane came down near Battalion Headquarters. The Pilot was dead but the other Officer was taken prisoner by Lieut. W. Matthews (the first Prisoner). On 14th May the 33rd Battalion was relieved in the Le Touquet Sector, from the River Lys on the right to Lowndes Avenue on the left.

An enemy Raid was expected on this Sector. Fritz was very active with his "Pineapples" and "Reserve Farm" was heavily shelled with "Minnies" each day, which made huge craters in the Line. "B" Coy. was only 50 yards from the enemy Front Line, with a small lake between them. Snipers were active on both sides and consistent shelling continued. Lewis Guns and Machine Guns were placed in position and everything put in readiness for the expected Raid.

At 8.45 p.m. on 17th May Fritz laid down an extremely heavy Barrage of "5.9's", "4.2's" and "Minnies". This extended from the right of Gap "A" to the left of Gap "F". All four Company Headquarters and Battalion Headquarters were subjected to extreme bombardment for three minutes. Communications and Back Areas were swept with a Machine Gun Barrage. At 8.50 p.m. the Barrage was taken off the Right and Left Flank and concentrated on Locality "C" Gap "D". At 8.55 p.m. the Barrage lifted off the Front Line and the enemy rushed Gap "D" in two small columns, with an estimated strength of 80 to 100 men. Lieut. J. Waugh, on duty at the time, put up the S.O.S. Signal. Our Artillery gave an excellent counter Barrage within 10 seconds and the Raid was successfully repulsed. None of the enemy succeeded in entering our Trenches. The N.C.O. leading the left party of enemy Raiders reached our parapet, but was shot by Lieut. J. Waugh and Pte Kirk, a Lewis Gunner, who displayed conspicuous bravery. Lieuts. J. Waugh and H. McLeod displayed great gallantry and were recommended for the Military Cross. Our casualties were 4 killed and 21 wounded. The enemy Barrage having died down somewhat, Lieut. B. Brodie with the Battalion Scouts searched No Man's Land but failed to obtain any identifications. Owing to the severity of the Barrage all communications with the Companies were destroyed, and Company Runners did particularly fine work in keeping up communication with Battalion Headquarters, the "D" Coy. Runner having to travel 3,000 yards.

At 8.50 p.m. on 18th May the enemy put down a heavy Box Barrage on "D" Coy., while intense fire was also maintained over the remainder of the area. The enemy attacked in three waves of about 200 men. Lieut. W. Edmonds, the Officer on duty, fired the S.O.S. Signal at 9.5 p.m. Our Artillery replied with a beautiful Barrage which came down in seven seconds and caught the rear wave of the raiders. Five of the enemy succeeded in penetrating our lines and bombed one of our Lewis Gun teams, wounding four. The remaining two, Corporal Ham and Pte Taylor, continued to work the Gun and killed all five of the enemy. The remainder were completely demoralised by Rifle, Lewis Gun and Machine Gun Fire and withdrew leaving many wounded and dead in No Man's Land. Lieut. B. Brodie with the Battalion Scouts searched No Man's Land and after a sharp brush drove off two enemy patrols who were acting as covering parties to Stretcher Bearers who were endeavouring to take back their killed and wounded. One wounded

Fritz was taken prisoner and 11 identifications were obtained from the killed. The Raiders were from the 3rd, 4th and 5th Bavarian Regiments, part of the 16th Bavarian Division. We killed between 25 and 30 of the enemy. Immediately the Barrage opened communications were cut and Runners had great difficulty in maintaining communication between the Front Line and Headquarters. One Runner was blown to pieces bringing the confirmation of the S.O.S. Corporal A. J. Grunsell of "D" Coy. showed great bravery and volunteered four times to carry messages, passing through the Barrage on each occasion. For this he was later awarded the Military Medal. Lieut. Edmonds, who displayed great courage and by his coolness set a fine example to the men, was awarded the Military Cross. Corporal Ham was also recommended for the Distinguished Conduct Medal.

At 10 p.m. on 20th May the Battalion was relieved by the 36th Battalion and returned to Billets at Pont de Nieppe. Whilst here the enemy continued to shell the area.

On 23rd May the Battalion moved to Billets in Ploegsteert Wood and took over from the 37th Battalion. After three days the 33rd Battalion was relieved in the Front Line. On 29th May we were relieved by 35th Battalion and moved back to Ploegsteert Wood, and supplied Working Parties for St. Andrew's Drive, Breastworks and Assembly Trenches. On 1st June a small silent Raid was made with 2 Officers, 2 N.C.O's and 24 men. The object was to kill the enemy, obtain identification and destroy Dugouts. The Raiders were divided into two parties. Lieut. E. Shannon with 12 men and 1 N.C.O. to enter the enemy Trench from the right and Lieut. B. Brodie with 12 men and 1 N.C.O. to enter the Trench from the left. Both parties were to work to the centre. This enterprise was successful but was marred by the death of Lieut. E. Shannon, a very gallant and efficient Officer. His party had entered the Trench without opposition, but after bombing the first Dugout was attacked by a party of the enemy who issued from the rear exit of a second Dugout. Lieut. Shannon was killed by a bomb thrown by one of this party. Our men immediately attacked the enemy and forced them back into the Dugout, where they were killed by our bombs, which were thrown in. The left party under Lieut. Brodie met with considerable opposition in passing through the enemy wire, but succeeded in entering the Trench and destroying two Dugouts and the occupants. It was now daylight and enemy opposition was increasing, so this party withdrew to our Front Line. The men in Lieut. Shannon's party displayed great determination and bravery in bringing back his body in broad daylight under heavy fire. Just previous to being relieved on 2nd June by 11th Brigade, Headquarters were destroyed by enemy fire. The Battalion marched to Billets in Nieppe and supplied Working Parties and did general work in preparation for the Messines Offensive. During this period the enemy shelled the village and there was a general exodus of civilians. Lieut. J. Waugh was wounded on a Working Party here. A number of our Ammunition Dumps were blown up by enemy fire at Hyde Park Corner. During this period the Battalion was equipped for the Messines Battle. The equipment carried was as follows:—

Each man carried a Rifle and Bayonet (except No. 1 Lewis Gunners, who carried Revolvers, Ammunition and Lewis Gun), Haversack on back, containing Cardigan and Jacket. 24 Hours' Rations, Waterproof Sheet, Spare Oil Tin, 6 Sand Bags, Small Arms Ammunition (Bayonet Men 220 Rounds; Lewis Gunners, Bombers, and Rifle Grenadiers 120 Rounds; Signallers, Runners, and Carrying Parties 50 Rounds each). Mills Hand Grenades 1 in each top pocket of tunic. These to be used only in emergency. 1 Aeroplane Flare in lower pocket of tunic for each man in fighting Line and Box Respirator at alert, Water Bottle filled. Extra glass bottle of water. Bayonet men in Second Wave carried Pick and Shovel. Lewis Gunners, except No. 1, carried five magazines. Bombers carried throwers and five bombs each. Bayonet men 10 and Carriers 15 bombs each in a bag at left side. Rifle Grenadiers carried 8 Grenades, 5 Spare Rods and 5 Blank Cartridges in Sand Bag at left side. Wire Cutters were carried by men of the First Wave.

S.O.S. Rockets, 12 were carried by Company Headquarters. Artillery Discs carried by an N.C.O. or man in each Platoon. Patches of colour were worn for identification purposes as follows:—"A" Coy., Red; "B" Coy., Blue; "C" Coy., Yellow, "D" Coy., Green. This colour patch was sewn on the back of the Tunic below the collar. Bands were worn around the left forearm as follows:—Scouts, Green; Runners, Red; Regimental and Company Signallers, Blue; Carrying Parties, Yellow; Mopping Up Parties, White; Salvage, Khaki, with Salvage in Red; Wire Cutters or Breakers, White Tape on shoulder strap.

BATTLE OF MESSINES

At 10 p.m. on 6th June, 1917, the Battalion left its Billets fully equipped for the assembly Trenches. The order of march being—"D", "A", "C", and "B" Companies. All went well until just before reaching Gunners Farm, where the enemy was putting a number of Gas Shells over and Masks had to be put on. Ploegsteert Wood and the back areas were receiving particular attention. All Companies were greatly delayed on account of the amount of Gas in the Wood, which resulted in a number of men being gassed on the way up and many others being completely exhausted. A number of men lost their way in the darkness and smoke. Many could not see at all and had to be led by their comrades. In many cases it was the blind leading the blind. After a gruelling March, the first arrivals reached the Assembly Points 30 minutes before Zero Hour, while the last Company arrived only 10 minutes before Zero. On 7th June, seven seconds before Zero Hour, which was 3.10 a.m., four Mines on our Front were fired. There was a violent swaying as if an earthquake had taken place and men in many instances were thrown together. The sky was brilliantly illuminated by the explosives and terrific Artillery Fire, the sound of which could not be heard above the intense Machine Gun Barrage.

The men left the Trenches immediately and there were a number of casualties on the parapet owing to the heavy enemy Barrage. The supports were also being heavily shelled and the Reserve Company ("D") suffered considerable losses. The weather was hot and sultry and every one felt the trying march.

The Battalion passed through the 35th Battalion in the vicinity of the enemy's original Front Line, near Ulster Switch. The enemy fire had been very severe up to this point and many men were lying here. A halt in our Barrage gave the Company Commanders an opportunity of checking their Compass Bearings, defining their limits, and getting into position for the next advance. At the lift of the Barrage a fine assault in complete waves was made. The men gained their objective in fine style behind a perfect Barrage and commenced consolidating their position. The mopping up of the Trench System was soon accomplished and many of the enemy were killed in their Dugouts. By 5.30 a.m. fair cover had been obtained on the Consolidation Line. At 6.30 a.m. Enemy Machine Guns were located in a redoubt in "Uncertain Trench" and heavy Artillery fire was brought to bear on them with good results. By 7.30 a.m. the Black Line was down to two-thirds of its depth and linking up by Companies and Platoons was in progress. The enemy was seen moving along "Uncertain Trench" and also reports were received from the 33rd Battalion that the enemy was massing 1,000 yards in front. Reports of enemy movement continued throughout the early part of the morning, but Artillery co-operation helped to disperse the tendency and during the day no organised counter attack was attempted.

At 8.30 a.m. the Line was well dug along the Front and affording excellent protection for the men. By 9.30 a.m. only one gap remained between "A" and "B" Companies in the full length of the Consolidation of the "Black Line" to the River La Douve. The Trenches being now well down, widening and sandbagging were now in progress and at 11.30 a.m. showed very plainly in an Aerial Photo as a good defensive Trench. There were repeated enquiries for water from the Front Line. Carrying Parties were suffering heavy casualties and were completely knocked up with the long distances.

At 1.40 p.m. Capt. A. Whitlock with "D" Company advanced to the Green Line, without Artillery support, owing to an alteration in the Zero Hour not reaching him. At 2.45 p.m. he reported by Runner that, having waited 30 minutes and no Artillery Barrage as arranged having been put down, he had advanced to the Green Line and was consolidating. By 7.30 p.m. all Companies reported that their positions were well consolidated.

Just before midnight Capt. A. Whitlock was killed between the Green and Black Lines, and Capt. R. J. Stewart took command of "D" Company. Patrols under the Scout Officers went out during the night and encountered enemy Patrols which were dispersed. A number of enemy Patrols were also killed by our Machine Gun and Lewis Gun fire earlier in the night. At 5.0 a.m. on 8th June an enemy Plane came over, flying low and inspected our new positions. Our casualties to date had been 8 Officers and 236 Other Ranks. Capt. A. Whitlock and Lieut. L. Warner K.I.A.; Lieuts. W. Matthews, H. McLeod, B. McKenzie, B. Brodie, T. Pittaway and F. W. Walker wounded.

During the morning the enemy put over a heavy Barrage of 7.7's and 4.5's. Capt. Stewart sent a message by pigeon that our own Heavies were dropping a few Shells short and doing some damage to our Trenches and causing a few casualties. Several messages were sent back but it was some time before the matter was rectified. At midday enemy Machine Gun Fire from the vicinity of Potterie Farm, about 300 yards from our Front, was very troublesome. At 4 p.m. our Artillery opened up a heavy bombardment which continued for four hours. This was replied to by the enemy at 8.30 p.m. and was particularly heavy north of La Douve. Ten minutes after this opened all communication lines were cut and messages were sent on the Power Buzzer. By 10.40 p.m. everything had become normal and the night was fairly quiet.

On 9th June Lieut. C. Jeffries with a Patrol of 50 Other Ranks left our Trenches at 4.0 p.m. with the object of reconnoitring Potterie Farm. This Patrol came under heavy Machine Gun fire and on returning reported the position was fairly strongly held. Lieut. Jeffries was wounded, 2 Other Ranks killed and 3 wounded.

At 2 a.m. on 10th June the Battalion was relieved by the 36th Battalion and proceeded to Breastworks at "Bunhill Row" and "Prowse Tunnels". Three days were spent resting in the "Wood". The enemy shelled heavily the whole time, day and night, with H.E. and Gas Shells, causing a number of casualties. Aircraft was also active on both sides.

On the night of 12th June the Battalion moved out to Vauxhall Camp and was here reinforced by reserve men from Morbecque. The whole operation had been most successful, in spite of the difficult approach March, caused by the wearing of Gas Masks and the darkness of the night. About 3.30 a.m. an unusual occurrence happened when one of our Planes, flying low for observation, was struck by one of our Shells and was cut in halves. During the whole period rations were taken up as usual, the limbers and Carriers being constantly under heavy fire. Many brave deeds were performed and a number of Officers and men were recommended for decorations which were in many cases awarded later. Total casualties were 10 Officers and 399 Other Ranks.

On 14th June the Battalion moved to billets near Vieux Berquin for rest and training. Next day the Corps Commander, Lieut.-General Sir A. J. Godley, inspected the Battalion at Doulieu. Capt. C. W. Bean, Australian War Correspondent, was also present.

The following day General Plumer, Army Commander, interviewed the Officers and addressed them. The weather was fine and the men had a good time bathing, writing letters and resting, while reorganisation and training was also carried out.

On 21st June the Battalion moved back to Vauxhall Camp and the following day went into tents at Neuve Eglise and relieved 1st Wiltshire Regiment.

Training, sports and other competitions were carried out. The weather was fine and enemy planes were very busy strafing our Observation Balloons and the Artillery on several occasions shelling Neuve Eglise. Whilst here the Duke of Connaught held an Inspection at Bailleul, the Battalion being represented by Capt. R. J. Stewart, Coy. Sgt. Major T. Norman and 3 Other Ranks.

On 27th June a Sports Day was held and the enemy livened up the proceedings by setting fire to four of our Balloons at the one time. During the evening the Cooees gave a concert. A 9 p.m. the same evening the Battalion marched to Messines to the rear of Middle Farm and relieved the 36th Battalion in reserve. From here the Battalion supplied Working Parties during the night time. The enemy shelled continuously and there were a number of casualties. The Transport had a very difficult time taking up the Rations along the track which was being continuously shelled, especially in the gully near the Railway Line.

On 1st July at about 4.30 a.m. the Transport came under heavy shell fire and Sgt. T. Malone, who was in charge, called a halt for a time. When things appeared a little quieter he decided to make a dash for the Ration Dump. When about 300 yards from it a heavy Shell struck the Transport, killing Sgt. Malone and a Storeman and wounding three others. The Limber was upset into a hole and the Mules killed. The wounded having been taken back, the Rations were delivered to the Battalion, good work being done by Pte A. J. Taylor. The weather was fine but the ground was a mass of Shell Holes. Continual trouble was experienced in transporting Rations, as the enemy appeared to have good observation and always seemed to open fire on any movement. Carrying Parties had long trips to make and heavy loads to carry and were under constant Shell fire. Tracks were changed but conditions did not improve and numerous casualties were sustained nightly. Lieut. H. Bennett, who had charge of the

Carrying Parties, did good work under trying circumstances and by his coolness set the men a fine example.

On the night of 3rd July the Battalion relieved the 33rd Battlion at Middle Farm. Lieut. H. Lilja joined here with a number of reinforcements. The enemy was raining Shells on this position, but it was very noticeable that a large percentage were "duds", as many as 15 in succession.

The Battalion was relieved by the 36th Battalion on 6th July, and on 7th July during the afternoon Lieut-General Godley held a review at Hillside Camp. Capts. R. Stewart and H. Percy were decorated with the Military Cross Ribbon, while 1 Distinguished Conduct Medal and 11 Military Medal Ribbons were presented to Other Ranks. Rain and heavy shelling made conditions bad, but the weather cleared later and Air Fights became more frequent, with sometimes as many as 30 enemy Planes in one formation.

On 12th July the Battalion relieved the 44th Battalion in the Front Line. This was carried out with great difficulty owing to heavy enemy Arillery Fire. On the night of 13th July the enemy opened up a heavy bombardment on our Front Line. Capt. Stewart, "A" Coy., sent up the S.O.S. Signal and a good response was made by our Guns, but no enemy movement followed. However, early in the morning many Bombs were thrown into "A" Company's Trenches from a Strong Point opposite "Gapaard Avenue".

The Trenches were very wet and muddy, with water in some places two feet deep. Ration Carriers had considerable difficulty in getting through. Duckboards were floating about in the Trenches. Rain continued to fall and conditions became worse, making the Trenches miniature canals. Heavy shelling was put over by the enemy, day and night, around "Gapaard" and "Wellington" Avenues, also "Owl" Trench, causing great damage to our Trenches.

Our 4.5 Howitzers put up a four-hour Barrage to destroy three enemy Strong Posts, which were causing trouble to "A" Company by throwing Bombs and small calibre "Minnies" into our Trenches, with resulting casualties. A Raid was planned for the night, but as the Howitzer Barrage failed to destroy the Strong Posts, Capt. Stewart sent a message asking that it be postponed. However at 9.15 p.m. instructions were received from Brigade to go on with the enterprise. At 10 p.m. Lieut. G. Hodges and 45 Other Ranks with two Lewis Guns attacked the Strong Posts. Immediately the party left the Trench they were met with a Barrage of Machine Gun Fire, Bombs and Grenades, from these Posts. The men pressed on with great determination until Cinema Road was reached. Here enfilade Machine Gun Fire was brought to bear on them by the enemy who, it was discovered, were standing shoulder to shoulder under good cover waiting to attack. Lieut. Hodges successfully arranged the withdrawal of his Party under difficult circumstances. At 10.58 p.m. the enemy heavily bombarded our Front and Support Lines and gave every indication of an immediate attack. Capt. Stewart fired the S.O.S. and the answering Barrage prevented the development of the attack. Our casualties in this operation were 2 killed and 10 wounded. The Stretcher Bearers did some good work under heavy fire and succeeded in bringing in our wounded.

The Battalion was relieved by 36th Battalion on 17th July and moved to a position of support in "Huns Walk" and the Subsidiary Lines in front of Messines. During the progress of the relief the enemy sent over a great quantity of Mustard Gas, which made the change over both difficult and most unpleasant. There were no serious casualties, but a number of men were slightly gassed. Shelling of this area continued during the night of 18th/19th July, with large quantities of both H.E. and Gas Shells. Also large formations of enemy Aircraft were constantly flying overhead. From here Working Parties were supplied for the Front Line and Jumping Off Trenches. While holding this Sector, all "B" Company's Cooks were killed. The Cook Houses were constantly under fire, as apparently the enemy was able to see the smoke issuing from them. Gapaard Avenue was also under constant Shell Fire, which caused many casualties. The whole of the Support area was under heavy fire from 5.9's and 4.2's, also Gas Shells. "C" Company at Zareete was subjected to an intense Barrage for two hours and sustained a number of casualties. Owing to the continuous Shelling some of the men were beginning to suffer from Shell Shock.

On the night of 23rd July the Battalion relieved the 36th Battalion in the Front Line Trenches, which were in a very bad state, from Staquart Farm to Bloumepuortbeck. It rained heavily most of the time, whilst the Shelling and Gas Barrages continued by night and day. On 26th July the Battalion moved back to "Huns Walk", where Working Parties were supplied for the Front Line. On 28th July the enemy put over a heavy Barrage from 10 p.m. until 5 a.m., along the whole of our Front and gave every appearance of a massed attack. The S.O.S. was called for and the Battalion stood in readiness for three hours, but the enemy did not follow up with an attack.

On 29th July the Battalion withdrew to Hillside Camp, near Waterloo Road. Heavy rain was still falling and making things generally unpleasant. The period of holding the Line at Messines was a very trying one. The enemy was in a good position and kept up a continual heavy bombardment of H.E. and Gas Shells. The Trenches, which were in very bad condition owing to the heavy rain, were under observation the whole time and special attention, by way of Shelling, was paid to the Cook Houses. The men were very tired after the strenuous period in the Trenches and were glad of a rest. While at Hillside Camp Working Parties were supplied and a general cleaning and refitting was carried out.

On 3rd August the Battalion marched out to Billets at Bleue via the Bailleul Road. The Billets were comfortable in old farms, but the rain continued and the roads were mostly under water. On the 5th a Brigade Church Parade was held and General Birdwood informally inspected the men. On 6th August the Battalion marched to Aldershot Camp. Whilst here Working Parties were supplied to dig a Corps Line in front of Messines. This entailed a long march to and from work, mostly under Shell Fire.

The Battalion left Aldershot Camp on 15th August and marched to Bailleul Station to entrain for Wizernes. From here a long march was carried out to Vaudringhem. This was quite a village and with its peaceful farms and green fields was a very pleasant change from the chaos of the Battle Area. The Billets were in old farm houses and the men trained with a zest and Sports were held twice weekly. New formations were practised and everyone was made ready and fit to again meet the enemy and defeat him.

On 27th August Brigadier-General Rosenthal took over the Brigade from Brigadier-General Jobson. Brigade and Divisional Sports and also Cooking Competitions were held. Leave was granted to Boulogne and the men were able to have a swim in the sea. A picnic by motor lorry to Boulogne was arranged and the men waited two hours with towels, when word came through that it was cancelled owing to shortage of lorries. Much to their disappointment, as other Battalions had made the trip.

On 26th September the Battalion left Vaudringhem at 6 a.m. and proceeded via St. Pierre, Elnes, Lumbres, Wizernes, Blendecques, Heuringhen to Coubronne. The Billets were very scattered over the villages of Coubronne, Islinghem, Le Rons, Blamart and La Sablon. It was a long march of 21 miles and the men were very tired, but fortunately the weather was fine and warm.

The following day leaving the Starting Point at 4 a.m. the March was continued via Quiestede, Wardrecques, Ebblinghem, Staple, Oxlaere, St. Marie Cappel, St. Sylvestre, Eecke to Godewaersvelde, arriving at 7.30 p.m. The men were done up after covering 23 miles, and glad to spend the night resting. On 28th September at about 8 a.m. a large barn near "B" Company Headquarters and the Q.M. Store caught fire and a considerable amount of straw and the roof were burnt. What caused the fire was never discovered but eventually the Battalion paid for the damage. Later that day the March was continued to Winnezeele via Steenvoorde, a distance of 8 miles, in lovely weather.

On 29th September the Battalion left for Zonnebeke. According to arrangements the C.O. and Adjutant went forward to the Line, followed by the Specialists who were taken by motor bus to Vlamertinghe and then marched to the Line via Menin Gate, Ypres and Railway Wood, where guides were met. The remainder of the Battalion went by motor bus via Abeele, Poperinghe, Dickebusch to Vlamertinghe and then marched into the Line. Our Front was from Brick Kiln south of Zonnebeke Station to Vanisackers Farm. The 35th Battalion being on the right and the 36th on the left. The Units relieved were what remained of the Northumberland Fusiliers, Gordon Highlanders, Welsh Fusiliers and King's Own Regiment. The Q.M. Store and Transport proceeded to Brandhoek and the "B" Teams to Morbecque.

Battalion Headquarters was at Low Farm. Aircraft was very active and the enemy heavily bombarded the Ypres-Zonnebeke Road, apparently searching for our Artillery positions. A quantity of Mustard Gas Shells were fired into Railway Wood and the Frezenberg Ridge. The enemy bombing Planes were constantly dropping bombs on all camps and roads, taking advantage of the clear moonlight nights. On

30th September our Support Line was subjected to heavy shelling by 7.7's, 5.9's and 4.2's at 9.30 p.m., which gave a cable burying party an intense straffing, resulting in 51 casualties.

On 1st October the enemy put down a heavy barrage of 5.9's and 4.2's on "A" Company from 7 a.m. to 9.30 a.m., badly knocking about our half-made Trenches. Lieut. S. R. Callaghan was killed and there were 53 casualties among the Other Ranks. Enemy Planes were flying low over our Lines and Machine Gunning the Trenches.

On 3rd October at 8.30 a.m. the enemy shot up Potsdam, Bowry Farm, Low Farm and Frost House with H.E., but no material damage was done to the Battalion. Relief by the 10th Brigade took place that night and the Battalion marched back to the Ramparts of Ypres, after having had a strenuous time in the Line. However the enemy Planes were busy bombing Camps, Roads and Transport and many casualties were suffered. On 4th October at 10.30 a.m. the Battalion marched from the Ramparts to No. 16 Central Camp, south of Ypres — a tent camp — arriving at noon. The move was made after a successful attack had been carried out at 6 a.m. by the 10th and 11th Brigades. A Working Party of 100 men which had been sent to prepare an Artillery Road to Seine House, was badly shot up at about 4.30 p.m. and had to cease work. The enemy Planes that night, again active over our Camp, dropped their quota of Bombs.

On 5th October the Troops were moved by Motor Bus to Winnezeele and reached Camp at 7.30 p.m. The Transport and Q.M. Stores marched in at midnight from Brandhoek. The motor lorry conveying the Packs capsized in a ditch, but they arrived during the early morning. The "B" Teams marched in from Morbecque. Cleaning up and organising for the 3rd Battle of Ypres was carried out during the four days spent at this Camp which consisted of Tents.

On 10th October the Battalion moved by Motor Bus to the Camp Area at Cavalry Farm, East of Ypres, arriving at 9 p.m. and spent the night in the open as no arrangements had been made for Billets. Some difficulty was experienced in getting to the allotted areas, as the night was dark and each party arriving would make for the nearest flame of a Cooker. However by 11 p.m. the men had been fed and were doing their best to settle down in the open, in spite of the heavy rain and cold as well as enemy Bombs. The enemy on the crest of the hill ahead of Passchendale must have plainly seen the fires in the Cookers and anticipated activity in this area, as early next morning Planes were over taking in the general situation.

On 11th October the Second in Command and other Officers reconnoitred the ground of attack for the following day. The weather was still showery and misty and the men rested while the Band played selections during the day. Lieut. T. C. Pittaway, Scout Officer, and Company Officers went up during the afternoon to lay the tape and were heavily shelled. The men were given a good tea, after which the various equipment for the operation was issued to them.

BATTLE OF YPRES

The Approach March commenced at 6 p.m. from Cavalry Camp to the jumping off Line, the Assembly Point being the Junction of Zonnebeke-Roulers Railway Line and Cemetery to the South West corner of Augustus Wood, thence to Assembly Road along Roulers-Ypres Railway Line.

The march was carried out without loss for about 7 Kilos, although the going was extremely difficult due to the rain and shell-holed state of the track, until Zonnebeke Station was reached. From here to the Assembly tape the Battalion was subjected to heavy shell fire, principally 7.7's and 4.2's, in many places the track had been blown up and the tape had disappeared. However in spite of this and casualties sustained, the Assembly Point was reached by 2.45 a.m. on 12th October, but some men were still arriving at Zero Hour. The heavy shelling of the 7.7's and 4.2's continued during the Assembly and right up to Zero Hour, the greater part of which appeared to come from the South and South East of Passchendale. Our casualties were very heavy, principally on the right flank near the cemetery and mostly occurred in "A" and "B" Companies.

The Brigade was formed up on the jumping off tape in the following order — 34th, 35th and 36th Battalions. The 35th and 36th Battalions suffered heavily and were badly shot up, as the shells were passing over the 34th Battalion and were falling on the two rear Battalions.

At 5.25 a.m. our Barrage came down, but was so weak that in many cases it was difficult to determine which was our Barrage and which was the enemy's. This made it hard for the men to keep up with the Barrage, however the greatest obstacle met in the advance was the condition of the ground, particularly on the left flank of "C" and "D" Companies. There were many men lost altogether in the mire. The pace of the advance was slowed up owing to the assistance it was necessary to give men who had sunk into the shell holes and could not extricate themselves without assistance. In a number of cases the helpers became engulfed in the awful morass and many of the wounded had to be left where they fell. The first organised opposition met with was two concrete Pill Boxes, East of Augustus Wood and North East of Seine House. These held up the centre of the advance until Capt. C. Jeffries organised a Bombing Party and succeeded in rushing and capturing the Strong Point, taking 35 Prisoners and Four Machine Guns. 150 yards in the rear of this Dugout was a small Trench, about 50 yards long, in which were 20 or 30 of the enemy, who were accounted for as the Wave passed on. Throughout the advance to the Red Line heavy M.Gun Fire was encountered from the direction of Belle Vue and Meetchiele on the left flank, and from Tiber and Tiber Copse on the right flank. Two M.Guns were firing from Deding Copse on the right flank in the Railway Embankment. This position was also mopped up as the Wave went forward. On reaching the Red Line the Battalion began to dig in, but was greatly harassed by fire from Machine Guns situated on the right flank, about 200 yards from the Railway Embankment. Capt. C. Jeffries again organised a Party of 2 N.C.O's and 10 men to capture this Post. Unfortunately this brave Officer was killed in the attempt. (For this action he was posthumously awarded the Victoria Cross.)

The N.C.O's carried on and captured the Post after a gallant fight, taking two Machine Guns and 40 Prisoners. Casualties all along had been very heavy and the 35th and 36th Battalions had also suffered severely. It was decided to send all men of the 34th Battalion to assist in the capture of the Blue and Green Lines. Capt. J. W. Richardson of "D" Company succeeded in reorganising the Battalion and took them forward to the Blue Line, where he was killed. Tiber Copse caused considerable trouble, but was taken by organised Parties of the 35th and 36th Battalions, augmented by the 34th Battalion. On reaching the Blue Line, the Parties commenced to dig in and were subjected the whole time to heavy Machine Gun Fire from Belle Vue and Meetchiele, in addition to heavy Barrage Fire from the enemy's Artillery. At 3 p.m. word was received that owing to the severity of hostile Shelling and Machine Gun Fire the Line was withdrawing. Instructions were immediately sent to hold the Line at all costs and to endeavour to refuse the left flank. Under a murderous fire and the vilest conditions a new Line was constructed from Deine Crossing on the Ypres-Roulers Railway, north to the direction of Waterfields. In the advance to the Red Line all the Officers of the Battalion had been either killed or wounded with the exception of three, who became casualties before reaching the Blue Line. Therefore the bulk of the organisation fell on the shoulders of the N.C.O's, who, although suffering heavy casualties, did remarkably fine work. The Trench Mortars took no active part in the Battle. One Mortar was blown out before reaching the Assembly Line and owing to the difficulties of the ground the Ammunition Carriers of the other did not arrive. The Machine Gunners found it impossible to carry their Guns forward and they did not arrive at the Assembly Point until some hours after Zero. The general condition of the ground over which the men had to travel and attack was one of the two primary causes for the non-success of the operation. Never before had men been called upon to fight under such awful conditions. It was simply a mass of mud and water across the entire Front. A succession of water-filled Shell holes, which not only reduced the rate of advance but bunched the men together in their attempt to find a track around the Shell holes. This gave the enemy a splendid opportunity to use his Machine Guns. The Barrage throughout was very weak, no doubt caused by the extreme difficulty experienced in getting the Guns and Ammunition forward owing to the terrible state of the ground. Thus many enemy Strong Points which otherwise would have been put out of action, were left to take active participation in the fight. Belle Vue on the left flank gave the enemy a magnificent field of Fire across the whole Brigade Front. Failure may have been turned to success if the Reserve Battalion had been brought up and used to reinforce the other Battalions. Undoubtedly this would have been of great assistance on the Blue Line, in refusing the left flank and may have saved a withdrawal.

During the initial attack Battalion Headquarters were established at Seine House. An arrangement which worked well and proved economical for Signallers and Runners throughout. The following day, 13th October, the enemy kept up a heavy concentrated Artillery Fire over the whole area, apparently having no idea of the actual position of our troops. Seine House and the Regimental Aid Post at the Railway Line were subjected to particularly heavy Fire and many casualties occurred at both places. Major G. R. Clarke, R.M.O., was killed by a Shell which fell right amongst the wounded who were being dressed in the open. Major Clarke fell dead across an Officer of the 37th Battalion, whose wounds he was dressing. A number of the A.M.C. Staff were also killed and wounded by the same Shell. Capt. N. H. Bridge later took over as R.M.O. The Battalion was sadly depleted and all the Officers had become casualties. The "B" Team, consisting of 3 Officers and 135 Other Ranks, was sent forward as reinforcements. The Lewis Guns and Rifles were in a very bad state, as the liquid mud had gradually worked into the parts and put them out of action. The heavy Shelling continued, especially in the vicinity of the Railway and Seine Mule track. Great difficulty was experienced in getting the Rations up, as many of the Mules were being bogged and in some cases had to be abandoned. Enemy Planes were coming over in large formations, flying low and Machine Gunning both Troops and Transport, thus inflicting many casualties.

At 6 p.m. on 14th October, being relieved by the 43rd Battalion, the men in a very exhausted condition withdrew to the reverse side of Abraham Heights, as close support, whilst Headquarters remained at Seine House. Squadron after Squadron of enemy Planes continued to come over during the day and night, bombing and Machine Gunning with impunity, as our Planes were missing.

On the night of 15th October the Battalion relieved the 41st Battalion in the Front Line, from Augustus Wood to Waterfields, Batalion Headquarters being at Otto Farm. The 33rd Battalion was on our right and the Otago Rifles (N.Z.) on our left. The weather was bitterly cold and raining. About 100 Gas Shells came over but did little damage owing to the rain. Very heavy Shelling by 5.9's and 4.2's was systematically carried out as well as bombing by Planes. Everyone was having a very trying time, including the Q.M. Store and Transport at Caralong Farm. The Battalion was relieved on 19th October by the 4th Yorks and Lancs and marched to the Camp South Ypres. The Central Camp had been removed from Caralong Farm owing to the severity of Shelling. The men (a small number) arrived at Camp completely exhausted and done up. After a hot meal, rum and a complete change of clothing, the men settled down for a rest. However very little rest was obtainable, as Bombing Planes were freely dropping their cargoes on the Camp and surrounding area, day and night.

The total number who took part in this Operation, as far as the 34th Battalion was concerned, was 19 Officers and 509 Other Ranks.

Of these 16 Officers and 250 Other Ranks were either killed or wounded. The Officers killed in action were:—Major G. R. Clarke (R.M.O.), Capts. C. S. Jeffries and J. W. Richardson; Lieuts. J. W. Longworth, B. G. McKenzie, J. C. Burges and A. E. Watson. The Officers wounded were:—Capt. T. G. Gilder; Lieuts. A. L. Watson, T. C. Pittaway, C. O. Edwards, H. W. Lilja, E. C. Edwards, O. P. Davidson, W. C. Purvis, and G. Maitland.

At 11 a.m. on 21st October half of the Battalion entrained at Ypres and proceeded to Wizernes. Having detrained, marched via Lumbres and St. Pierre to Vaudringhem. The remainder embussed at Hell Fire Corner, after having waited three hours for the buses. During the wait two enemy Planes came over and having apparently spotted the concentration of Troops, within an hour the enemy opened up fire with his H.V. Rubber Gun. The last Bus had just crossed the Railway Line when a Shell burst right on top of a Staff Car and one burst on the road between the line of Buses. Having debussed about 3 Kilos from Vaudringhem, the men marched into that village. This was the second term there and the men settled down into fairly good Billets. From 22nd October until 9th November the Battalion remained at Vaudringhem, carrying out training and reorganisation for the next Offensive. The weather was mostly wet and windy.

On 9th November the Battalion marched to Drionville Cross Road and proceeded by bus to the Billeting Area at Bleu. At this stage the Division was attached to the 1st Anzac Corps. On 15th November the Battalion marched via La Verrier, Steenwerck, Rabot to Le Rossicuol Camp, North West of Nieppe. Whilst here cleaning up and training for Raids were carried out.

At 4.30 p.m. on 21st November the Battalion left the Camp and marched via Ploegsteert to Keepers Hut and relieved the 36th Battalion in the Front Line. The Trenches were in a very bad condition, with mud waist high in places. The Front Line from Posts 21 to 17 was practically impassable, whilst the same applied to Posts 16 to 15. Some 200 yards of Unpere Drive South was also impassable and it was necessary to go overland. In this Sector the enemy had many Observation Balloons and his Planes frequently flew over. Heavy Artillery and Minnie Barrages did constant damage to our Trenches and Ration Dumps, whilst Working Parties in Unpere Drive South sustained many casualties. Gas Shells were continually falling during the night, particularly on Convent Lane, Ayr Street and Una Avenue. Shelling was also heavy in the vicinity of Le Bizet and Ploegsteert Wood. During the night No Man's Land and Pont Rouge were patrolled by our Battle Patrols.

At 7.55 p.m. on 27th November a party of the enemy about 30 strong endeavoured to silently raid our Trenches at 21 Post. The Lewis Gunners caught them in the wire and, firing on them, forced them to retire. A Party under Lieut. R. Brown went out to clear up the situation, but was bombed by a second Party of the enemy from an old Trench in front of 21 Post. As this Party of the enemy retired through Pont Rouge, it was engaged by Lieut. T. Pittaway and four

Scouts, but there were too many of them to be cut off. He called on Lieut. H. Richardson, who had 20 men and a Lewis Gun on the right flank of Pont Rouge as a Standing Patrol. This Patrol came into action and the enemy Patrol rapidly retired over the Pont Rouge Bridge, leaving one dead and several Rifles.

Being relieved by the 36th Battalion on 29th November, the Battalion returned to Le Rossicuol Camp, with the exception of 168 who remained behind as Working Parties in Fusilier Terrace.

On 5th December small circular enemy Balloons came over our Line and pamphlets in English and French were dropped from them, apparently by means of some mechanical contrivance. These pamphlets purported to be (a) from French inhabitants in occupied areas, giving casualties suffered by the civil population as a result of our Bombing and Artillery Fire; and (b) accounts of German successes and pointing out the helpless position of the Allies.

The Battalion remained here in support to the Pont Rouge Sector until 7th December, when the 36th Battalion was relieved by it in the Front Line. At dawn the enemy opened up a heavy strafe, which fell thickly on our Sector, as well as the Ration Dump and Ethelwood Hall. During the night 300 rounds of Gas Shells fell in the area. Our Patrols worked No Man's Land without sighting the enemy. On the night of 9th December our Front Line from Dolls House to Wicart Farm was swept with Machine Gun Fire and at 2 a.m. the enemy heavily shelled "A" Company Headquarters and did considerable damage to the Trenches. Three large Shells struck the Cook House and blew up most of the gear.

During the morning General Birdwood visited the Sector. In the afternoon visibility improved and the enemy put up 12 Observation Balloons. A Squadron of Planes flew over and dropped Bombs on the Camp and Transport Lines at Le Rossicuol and Romarin. On 11th December "C" and "D" Companies changed over from the Support to the Front Line, relieving "A" and "B" Companies. Just after noon next day a Squadron of enemy Planes flew over and again bombed the Camps at Le Rossicuol and Romarin. Five of our Planes attacked and brought down one of their Planes in flames in No Man's Land, on our Front to the right of Ida Post.

On 13th December the enemy put down a Box Barrage of H.E., extending from Ida Post, Una Avenue and Convent Lane to the 33rd Battalion on our right. No real damage resulted and an expected enemy Raid did not follow. On the following days enemy Planes were very active, and many Air Fights took place, one enemy Plane being brought down near Le Touquet Station.

Being relieved by the 18th Battalion on 15th December, the Battalion marched to Billets at Nieppe. After spending a night and day there, the Battalion marched to the Hutment Camp at de Seule and settled down to equipment cleaning. The following day was intensely cold and later snow fell. The Referendum on Conscription was held.

On 19th December the Battalion marched from de Seule Camp to the Laundries Erquinghem and billeted there, relieving the Royal

Welsh Fusiliers, as Reserve to Armentieres Defences. The weather was cold and frosty, which gave some of the troops an opportunity of trying their skill at skating.

Christmas Day was celebrated in good style and was made realistic by a fall of snow. Food was ample and all Ranks enjoyed a traditional meal, accompanied by a plentiful supply of Beer. Fuel was in good supply and fires were kept going during the long evenings. Whilst here Capt. J. Florance took over as Quartermaster from Lieut. F. Baulch, who became Quartermaster at Brigade School. On 1st January, 1918, New Year's Day, the Battalion was relieved by the 171st Brigade and proceeded to de Seule Hutment Camp. Owing to a hard frost the marching was difficult. On the following day the march was continued via Bailleul to Meteren Billeting Area, where the Billets were very scattered. While here the frost broke, making the roads very muddy and unpleasant for marching and transport. General Training was carried out, interspersed with Sports and Football Matches. During this period, Capt. R. J. Stewart left the Battalion to take up special duty in England. Capt. T. G. Gilder took over command of "A" Company and Lieut. D. Granter became Transport Officer.

On 18th the Battalion at one hour's notice was turned out for a practice "Defence of Meteren" and all Ranks gave a good account of themselves. During the stay here Picquets were supplied and also a Working Party to salvage dead timber from Ploegsteert Wood. A number of Lectures were given and Officers and N.C.O's attended a demonstration at Wisques Brigade School. On 26th January the Battalion proceeded by route march to Bulford Lines and the following day took over Strong Posts on the Corps Line. Battalion Headquarters and Details moving to Romarin Camp.

On 3rd February General Birdwood presented Ribbons and Medals to the men of the Battalion. The 33rd Battalion having relieved the men in the Strong Posts, they rejoined the balance at Romarin Camp. Lieut.-Col. E. Martin having gone on leave to England, Major W. Le Roy Fry assumed command. Working Parties were supplied for the strengthening of the Corps Line, Cable Laying and timber getting in Ploegsteert Wood.

On 25th February the Battalion moved out and was conveyed by light railway to Racine Dump, and then marched to the Sector south of La Douve River at Bas Warneton, to relieve the 40th Battalion in the Front Line. A Raiding Party was left at the Camp for the purpose of training. The Front Line consisted of a series of Strong Posts, the two on our Front being Furze Cottage, known as "Victory", and La Potterie Farm, known as "Watchful". The Battalion Front was a 2 Company Front. With 2 Companies in the Front Line, 1 in Support and 1 in Reserve. Standing Patrols were supplied and the Gaps patrolled, as well as No Man's Land each night. Wiring and general improvement of the defences were carried out. The weather was intensely cold with some snow. The enemy shelled our Sector, causing several casualties, including Lieut. A. B. York, wounded.

At 11.45 p.m. on the 3rd March a combined 9th Brigade Raid took place, which proved most successful. One Officer and 11 Other Ranks were brought back as prisoners. Our casualties were 3 wounded. The following night the Brigade Raiders again entered the enemy Trenches and succeeded in killing 40 of the enemy. This Raid however was not so successful as on the previous night. The Battalion losing one of its efficient Officers—.Capt. B. G. Brodie. These Raids were well organised and the men, who had been especially trained, were well equipped. On the second night 100 men of the Battalion took part. The object of the Raid was to blow up Dugouts and Tunnels. The Assembly Point was in front of the 33rd Battalion Outpost Line near No. 7 Post in front of the Sugar Refinery. Our men were in "C" Company of the Raiders, with Capt. B. G. Brodie in charge. Lieut.-Col. J. A. Milne, 36th Battalion, was in charge of the Brigade Raid. Each man carried three or four Bombs. Some were Rifle Grenadiers, others Lewis Gunners, some Bombers and also Bayonet Men. Most were dressed in Tommy Uniforms. The demolition Party carried special charges and detonators. It rained heavily during the march to the Assembly Point and the men enjoyed the hot Cocoa and Coffee supplied by the Y.M.C.A. on the way up.

The Barrage opened at 12.50 a.m. and 1 Officer and 4 Other Ranks went forward to lay the tape for direction. Seven minutes later the Covering Party went out to the left flank and laid in the enemy wire, 45 yards from his Trenches. This Party was armed with Lewis Guns, Bombs and Grenades and was in charge of Sgt. W. Mudford. The Main Raiding Party followed the tape and, passing through the gaps cut in the wire, entered the Trenches. Strong opposition was encountered from the enemy, with Grenades and Machine Gun Fire. Capt. B. G. Brodie while standing on the parapet, directing operations, was hit in the chest and side by Machine Gun bullets. Lieut. A. J. Fell and his Party proceeded up the Communication Trench, while Sgt. C. Nunn worked along the Front Line to the left. Much opposition was met, as the enemy was apparently waiting in strong force. After six minutes they withdrew, bringing Capt. Brodie out, who died on the way back. Lieut. A. E. Rees, who was in charge of another Party, also returned after doing good work. Shortly afterwards the Covering Party under Sgt. Mudford returned and the 33rd Battalion again took over the Post. Later the enemy retaliated with heavy Shell Fire.

During the afternoon enemy Planes were very active and a Squadron flew over. One of these Planes released a paper balloon carrying pamphlets. These were collected and sent to Divisional Headquarters. At 2.40 p.m. on 6th March Warneton Tower was brought down by the fifth shot of a 15-inch Gun, much to the delight of the Troops who heartily cheered its downfall.

On 7th March the Battalion, on being relieved by the 24th Battalion, marched to Hyde Park Corner and were then conveyed by light railway to Romarin Camp. The following day the men marched to Steenwerck and entrained for Desures. Having detrained, the Battalion marched to Billets at Le Wast, arriving at 11 p.m. on 9th March. The Billets were comfortable but somewhat scattered. The weather was fine and mild. The Transport travelled by road from Romarin Camp, arriving in grand condition and were complimented for their smartness. Training was carried out in the mornings, while the afternoons were devoted to sports. The men were given leave to Boulogne and St. Omer. A Brigade School was formed under Major W. Le Roy Fry and Major H. L. Wheeler became Commanding Officer of the Battalion.

On 22nd March the Battalion left Le Wast and after marching to Lottinghem, entrained for Abeele, where it arrived the next day and marched to Watou. That evening Orders were received to be prepared to move and that all surplus baggage, including Officers' valises, was to be dumped. Leaving Watou on 24th March the Battalion marched to near Abeele and embussed for Wallon-Cappel in the Sercus area. On arrival at Hazebrouck the men debussed and marched to La Belle Hotesse, and were under Orders to be ready to move at any moment.

ON THE SOMME

On 26th March the Battalion and Transport marched to Steenbecque Station and entrained for Doullens, where on arrival it procceded by route march via the Arras main road to Henn and billeted. The train journey was most uncomfortable, as the men were packed into trucks like sheep. Four Strong Posts were garrisoned near the village by "A" Company, in addition to Strong Posts occupied by the Royal Scots.

The morning of 27th March broke fine and cold and at 4 a.m. the Battalion marched to Thienes where it was met at 7 a.m. by the Brigade Omnibus Train and conveyed to Franvillers, arriving at 2 p.m. The enemy was sending over a few Shells and most of the civilians had left the village. Many of them were met hurrying along the roads with whatever things they could carry. Some had waggons, others carts, barrows and perambulators. Many were very aged and a lot of young children were with them. Quite a number of these people returned to the village when they saw the Australians arriving and others who had not left called out "It will be all well now, the Hun will not come any further".

An hour later the Battalion marched to within 1 Kilo of Heilly and rested in a gully near the Brickworks whilst awaiting Orders and the men had a hurried meal. Two enemy Planes flew over and dropped what appeared to be messages, but some of the men who were nearby and ran to pick them up discovered that they were Bombs. The Planes, which had our markings, opened fire with Machine Guns and wounded two English soldiers. One hour later the men moved through Heilly and occupied Trenches in the Corps Line. The enemy was shelling heavily now and there were some casualties. A few English Troops who were digging Trenches on the crest and had only one Machine Gun, were relieved. A Party of Scouts under Sgt. G. R. Johnston went out and worked from the Sugar Mills at Ribemont to the left for a distance of 400 yards, but no enemy was encountered. The men occupied this Line until 11 p.m., during which time they had a hot meal and then proceeded to Bonnay where they arrived at 4 a.m. on 28th March, very tired and rested all day. Local reports were that the enemy had passed through this village during the day, in armoured cars. Food and drink were plentiful and the Troops enjoyed themselves whilst they had an opportunity. On 29th March the C.O. and Officers reconnoitred the Aubigny-Vaux Line held by the 33rd Battalion and at 8 p.m. the Battalion marched to Cachy. As the enemy was expected to attack early in the morning, the men stood to in readiness until after daylight. Some heavy Shells were coming over and Aircraft were frequently having air fights. English Troops were coming back in some disorder, with remarks that Jerry was coming over the hill in mass formation. After stand down some of the men went into Villers Bretonneux and when returning to the Unit were stopped by British Cavalry.

On 30th March the Battalion marched from Cachy to Bois d'Abbe and bivouaced in readiness to go forward as Counter Attack Troops.

Rain was falling and the men got what improvised shelter they could. "B" Teams were sent to Blangy Tronville, where the Quartermaster's Store and Transport were also stationed. At 9.30 a.m. the Battalion moved up to a position of support to 33rd Battalion who were attacking on the North side of Bois de Hangard and Lancers Wood. The men moved in Artillery Formation with the C.O., Lieut.-Col. E. Martin, leading on his favourite grey horse. Everyone was subjected to heavy Shell Fire from the enemy, who was also shelling Hangard Wood with his Heavies. Here a number of English and Scottish Troops were met. "A" Company was sent forward to report to the 33rd Battalion. The O.C., Capt. T. G. Gilder, reconnoitred and found that "B" Company of that Battalion had suffered heavy casualties and that the enemy was still holding the ridge, and it was decided to attack the enemy's position. At 8 p.m. "A" Company moved forward in two waves and then having formed one wave the whole Company attacked the ridge, driving the enemy out of what was apparently his Picquet Line. The advance was continued and the enemy was driven out of his continuous Line at the point of the bayonet. At this point seven prisoners were taken and about 60 of the enemy killed or wounded. Several of our wounded had to be left, as the demand on the Stretcher Bearers had been heavy, but were brought in later during the night. Enemy Machine Gun Fire was heavy on the left and caused the death of Lieut. R. Parkes. This system was held for about two hours. In the meantime Patrols were sent out on the right flank to establish communication with the 33rd Battalion. These encountered heavy fire from enemy Posts behind our Line on this flank. Touch eventually being made, it was decided to move back about 250 yards and dig in to conform to the Line held by the 33rd Battalion, thus filling a gap of about 600 yards. At 1.30 a.m. the enemy appeared on the skyline advancing in extended order. This apparent Counter Attack was completely broken up by our Machine Gun and Lewis Gun Fire. "B" Company had also occupied a position in the Line but had no actual fighting. At 3 a.m. these were relieved by a Surrey Regiment and moved back to Cachy.

On 31st March the men rested in Cachy until the enemy Shelling caused casualties and the Battalion moved out and occupied a position in Bois d'Abbe, in readiness as counter attack Troops. Whilst here Orders were received to dig a succession of Posts East of the Wood. The enemy was now shelling the whole area very heavily and even the Food had to be served under Shell Fire. At 3 p.m. on 2nd April Orders were received to stand to for a Counter Attack from Dormart to Hangard Wood, but the Cavalry having cleaned up the situation, the attack was cancelled. Rain was falling and, with the continuous Shelling, conditions were most uncomfortable.

At 10.30 a.m. on 4th April the Battalion moved forward to a position of readiness to defend Villers Bretonneux on the North. Moving off again in Artillery Formation, "A" Company on the right, "B" Company on the left, "C" Company in Support and "D" Company in Reserve. The enemy was shelling the Railway Line and the Main Villers Bretonneux-Amiens Road. To avoid this the Battalion worked around the low ground and took up a position behind terraces. At 1.10 p.m. the locality was heavily shelled, during which Lieut.-Col. E. Martin, the Adjutant, Lieut. A. G. Farleigh and Major H. L. Wheeler, also several Runners and Signallers, became casualties. The Bombardment continued for over an hour, during which time the men suffered heavily. The Regimental Aid Post was also heavily shelled and many of the casualties, being Stretcher Cases, could not be moved. Capt. E. E. Watson, M.O., and his Staff performed gallant work in attending to the wounded under extreme difficulty, thereby saving many dangerously wounded cases. At 3 p.m. Major W. Le Roy Fry took command of the Battalion. A request was received from the 12th and 17th Lancers to supply Troops to stiffen up the Line in this vicinity. This could not be acceded to, as our role was Counter Attack. At 4.30 p.m. an Order was received from Brigade to withdraw to high ground in rear of the village, which gave a good field of Fire North and North West of Villers Bretonneux. Whilst moving to this position, a second Order was received to withdraw to the rear of the village, South of the Railway Line. At 5.10 p.m. instructions were received to establish a Line connecting the 33rd Battalion on our left and the Cavalry on our right. This was completed by 9 p.m.

The enemy had established a Line on high ground West of the Railway Bridge with strong Machine Gun Posts, from which he could enfilade our Line North of the Railway and also command the approaches to the village. The position had to be cleared up and the Battalion was detailed to do so, by attacking and capturing the Railway Bridge and consolidating a new Line 250 yards in front. Zero was at 1.0 a.m. on 5th April and the operation was entirely successful. "D" Company experienced very little opposition until the Bridge was reached, when the enemy endeavoured to outflank our right. However this Party was dealt with and the Bridge was taken. "C" Company experienced strong opposition along the Railway Line, but succeeded in mopping up the enemy. In the advance the Lewis Gunners fired from their hips and the rapid Fire seemed to completely demoralise the enemy. 12 Machine Guns, one Officer and 22 Other Ranks were captured. The Line was consolidated and the rest of the night passed quietly, the 33rd, 35th and 36th Battalions moving their Line forward to conform with ours. During the afternoon the enemy put over a heavy Barrage of "Whiz Bangs" and 5.9's. The Trenches which had been dug during the night were narrow and placed in Platoon Posts, were difficult to hit and only a few casualties resulted. The ground was extremely flat and it was impossible to have any communication with the Front Line during daylight.

On the night of 5th/6th April the Battalion was relieved by the 17th Battalion and marched to Bois d'Aquenne and dug in the side of the ridge for cover, the night being very cold and wet. The morning of 6th April was bright and clear and there was great activity in the air. Fights were frequent, with as many as 30 Planes on each side fighting it out. The Transport coming up with the Rations was getting a particularly warm time from the heavy Shelling. Whilst here dry socks and underclothing were obtained for the men from Villers Bretonneux. Despite the bad weather and heavy fighting during the last 12 days, the men were in fine fettle and their morale was excellent. On 7th April the men moved into Villers Bretonneux and billeted in cellars in the vicinity of the Cross Roads.

The enemy continued to shell the town during the afternoon and night and rain again began to fall. About noon on 8th April the enemy put over an exceptionally heavy Barrage, but the men being housed in cellars, very little damage was done. On the night of the 9th April the Battalion relieved the 19th Battalion in the Front Line, in the vicinity of Bois de Hangard. The enemy had Strong Posts out in front, which were protected by barb wire in the stubble. The ground in front was absolutely flat, giving a good field of Fire. During next day our area, as well as Cachy and Hangard Villages, was heavily shelled. The following three days, except for some Machine Gun Fire, were normally quiet. On 13th April, being relieved by the 17th Battalion, the Battalion moved to Support in Bois de Hangard and bivouaced there until 15th April, when it relieved the 10th London Regiment in Reserve in Bois d'Abbe.

On 17th April about 600 rounds of Gas Shells came over the Sector, but although things were most unpleasant, no great damage was done. On 18th another 1,000 Gas Shells fell. This time there were some casualties, whilst nearly all the men were more or less affected. Whilst here the improvement of the Defences was continued by the digging of Trenches and wiring.

On 20th April the Battalion was relieved at 2 p.m. and marched to Billets in Franvillers and settled down fairly comfortably. This gave the men a much needed rest and an opportunity to clean up equipment and clothing. The enemy sent over a few Long Range Shells during the day and night.

On 24th April a heavy Bombardment and Attack by the enemy on Villers Bretonneux took place and the Battalion was ordered to stand to in readiness to move at a moment's notice. However nothing eventuated. Working Parties were supplied for the improvement of the Heilly Defences.

On 30th April the 36th Battalion was disbanded and 2 Platoons were attached to our Battalion. Whilst here the Battalion was congraulated on its grand work in the attack on 4th April, by General Sir John Monash and Brig.-General C. Rosenthal. In addition to those already mentioned the following Officers, who were either gassed or wounded, were evacuated during April:—Lieuts. T. C. Pittaway, G. E. Hodges, T. Bellamy, E. Brunker, P. Beauchamp, F. Lee and G. Gifford.

On 1st May the Battalion relieved the 41st Battalion in the Front Line, North of Sailly Le Sec, in front of Morlancourt. "D" Company in the Picquet Line. "B" and "C" Companies in the Main Line and "A" in Reserve. During the night of the 4th, the Picquet Line was advanced about 500 yards and eight Posts were dug. Brig.-General C. Rosenthal and Lieut.-Col. White, who had come forward to inspect the operation, encountered an enemy Ration Party of 6, whom they captured after wounding two of them. The nights were very dark and our Ration Parties had great difficulty in locating the isolated Posts.

On 5th May "D" Company plus 2 Platoons of "A" Company and "B" Company plus 2 Platoons of "A" Company in conjunction with the 35th Battalion again advanced the Picquet Line, capturing about 100 Prisoners and Machine Guns. The success of the operation was greatly assisted by the bravery of the Signal Officer, Lieut. H. McLeod, who after the members of his Signal Staff had become casualties, in over 1,000 yards of line repaired 62 breaks.

At 9 p.m. on 6th May "C" Company moved forward to occupy a new line of Posts. Owing to the darkness touch was lost between Platoons and Nos. 9 and 10 were unable to advance due to wire obstacles and enemy Strong Posts. No. 11 Platoon came into contact with a cluster of Strong Posts and suffered a number of casualties without being able to eject the enemy from their position. The Platoon Commander, Lieut. S. H. Hubbard, collected his men and moved in a North Easterly direction and on reaching the Bray-Corbie Road, made contact with "B" Company, at 1.30 a.m. As there were no Trenches and the men were only occupying pot holes, he placed his Platoon in drainage holes beside the road, in order to cover "B" Company's flank with Lewis Guns. At 2 p.m. on 7th May this Platoon and one from "B" Company under Lieut. S. Nicklin attacked the enemy Pot Hole Line extending 150 yards South of the road. Capt. N. Cains ably assisted from his position on the road with Lewis Guns and Rifle Grenades fired by Lieut. H. Lilja on anything holding up the advance. A Stokes Mortar Barrage helped clear the enemy from his positions, with the result that the operation was entirely successful.

At 11 p.m. on the same day, "C" Company with 2 Platoons of "A" Company on the right and "D" Company with 2 Platoons of "A" Company on the left were to be the first wave in an attack on the enemy positions which had been the objective on the previous night. The second wave was "C" Company of the 33rd Battalion. The 2 Platoons of "A" Company which were to assist "C" Company got lost in the dark and did not arrive. "D" Company reached their objective, but Capt. E. Beaver finding his right flank exposed and not being able to gain touch with "C" Company, dropped his right flank back to the existing Picquet Line.

"C" Company having reached their objective, but finding their flanks exposed, Capt. H. McMinn decided to drop back, but in doing so, owing to the intense darkness, lost direction and the Company found themselves behind the enemy Line. At dawn, realising it was useless to attempt to force their way back, they surrendered. Lieut. R. S. Brown was mortally wounded during the advance, whilst Lieuts. A. J. Fell and L. McMahon were also taken prisoners.

At 11 p.m. on 8th the "B" Teams relieved "D" and "A" Companies in the Picquet Line. Lieut.-Col. W. Le Roy Fry was evacuated to hospital with gas burns and Lieut.-Col. H. F. White took over command.

On 9th May the weather was fine and clear, with the enemy's Snipers fairly active along the Front. Our Snipers, however, were getting in some good work also. During the night of the 10th Listening Posts were pushed forward to cover the relief of the Battalion by the 17th Battalion. The men marched to a terrace in Lahoussoye, where they bivouaced for the night, after having a hot meal which was more than acceptable after the very strenuous time in the Line. Next day the Battalion marched to Rivery, near Amiens, and went into Billets at Ecole Commudle. On 13th May Major F. G. Grant took over command of the Battalion, and on the 14th General Birdwood, Corps Commander, paid a visit, during which he talked to the men and complimented the Transport on their smart appearance. A most enjoyable time was spent in these Billets, which were ideal for a rest, in glorious hot and dry weather. Parades were held in the mornings, whilst the afternoons were devoted to various kinds of sport, boating, fishing and swimming. In the evening concerts were given by the "Cooees". A swimming carnival was held at the Amiens Baths and altogether a most enjoyable time was spent by all.

On 20th May Brig.-General C. Rosenthal, who was to become G.O.C. 2nd Division, attended a Brigade Parade and in addressing the men handed over the command of the Brigade to Lieut.-Col. H. A. Goddard.

Leaving Rivery on 21st May the Battalion marched to terraces at Villers Bretonneux, where the 48th Battalion was relieved, in a Reserve position. Next day the enemy shelled the position heavily, especially around Battalion Headquarters, but little damage was done. The weather continued fine and warm. The following day two French 6-inch Guns took up a position below our Cookers to carry out a special shoot on two Bridges opposite the French Sector. They moved out at 6 p.m. on 25th and within an hour the enemy replied with 5.9's, 4.2's and Gas Shells. During the bombardment Lieuts. J. Monfries and T. N. Learmont were badly wounded.

On 27th about 1,500 rounds of Gas Shells were sent over by the enemy, which drenched the whole area with Gas which remained strong for 12 hours, owing to the lack of wind. The next day the enemy Planes showed remarkable activity over our Lines and were apparently screening some operation behind their own Lines. They attempted to stop our Planes going over their Lines, but without success.

On 29th May the Battalion relieved the 35th Battalion in Support, and almost immediately came under heavy Shell Fire, resulting in the death of Lieut. Macfarlane and a number of other casualties. The weather continued fine and warm and our Working Parties, which were repairing Trenches, were at times badly shot up. On 31st Lieut. A. Dowding, who was in charge of one of these Parties, was mortally wounded.

On 1st June the enemy continued to drench our position with Gas Shells, when from 2 a.m. to 4.15 a.m. 6,000 rounds fell in the area. The following morning from 3.30 a.m. to 4.30 a.m. another 5,000 rounds fell in the same area, making nearly all the Dugouts untenable owing to the Gas vapour. At 1.45 p.m. the enemy put over a number of heavy Shells which wounded two American Soldiers who were attached to us for experience, and also Lieut. T. Britton, who later died of his wounds. For the next two or three days heavy Shelling continued, with Black Shrapnel bursting high in the air, but doing very little damage.

On 7th June the 35th Battalion was relieved in the Front Line. The first few days were fairly quiet, but heavy Shelling of the back areas was continuous. Our Transport coming up from Blangy Tronville had some exciting times under Shell Fire. At 2.30 a.m. on 8th June, in the intense darkness, one of our Patrols encountered a Patrol of 14th Battalion A.I.F., who were on the left of our Sector. Rifles and Bombs were used, resulting in two of the 14th Battalion and one of our men being wounded. The enemy continued to heavily shell the gully behind our Support Line but did no material damage, although the Cookers in the sunken road had several narrow escapes.

At 1.0 a.m. on 14th June a minor operation was carried out by Sgt. P. C. Mudford, D.C.M., M.M. The Stokes Mortars put over a heavy Barrage of 300 rounds and at a given signal switched to the flanks. The Party entered the Trench, killing one and taking two prisoners. The Raid only occupied seven minutes, the only casualty, unfortunately, being Cpl. Harper, killed. The enemy Trenches were found to be in good condition, about 6 feet deep, with a series of Posts joined by tunnels which served as Dugouts. There was no wire in front of the Trenches.

On 17th June the Battalion being relieved by the 33rd Battalion, took over from the 35th Battalion in Reserve. Black Shrapnel was now coming over fairly frequently, but bursting high in the air did practically no damage. However a few Shells did burst low, causing one or two casualties, the first of this kind in the area.

On 23rd June Lieut.-Col. E.E. Martin rejoined the Battalion and took over command from Major F. Grant who remained as 2nd in command. Air fights were now frequent over the Lines with sometimes two Planes coming down in flames at the same time. On 27th Lieut. F. D. Thomas was evacuated wounded. Being relieved on 28th June by the 20th Battalion A.I.F., the Battalion was conveyed by motor lorry to the Rivery Area and settled in Billets which were terrace banks, covered with shelters. The weather was fine and warm. The men were kept busy cleaning up equipment and clothing, whilst swimming and Sports were carried out, as well as boating and fishing. A Picquet of 2 Officers and 50 Other Ranks was supplied daily for duty in Amiens.

On 1st July Lieut.-Col. E. E. Martin, D.S.O., the Commanding Officer, addressed the Battalion on its work during its sojourn in France and presented Parchments, with the 4th Army Commander's compliments and congratulations to the recipients of Decorations — Capt. C. E. Watson, M.C., and Lieut. J. Bruce, D.C.M., M.M.

The Green Diamond Concert Party gave concerts daily in the Hospital St. Victor Rivery. Cricket Matches, a Swimming Carnival and Transport Competition were held and the Troops generally were having a good time.

Tactical Training schemes were practised. Lewis Gun instruction was carried out at the Citadel, Amiens, and practise attack with Tanks was held.

Whilst here a redistribution of Headquarters and Company Officers took place:—

"Headquarters".—2nd in C., Major F. Grant; Adj., Capt. H. Hicks; Signal Officer, Lieut. H. R. McLeod; Scout Officer, Lieut. S. R. Smith; Lewis Gun Officer, Lieut. J. Sneddon; Intelligence Officer, Lieut. T. Williams; Transport Officer, Lieut. E. C. Edwards; Q.M., Capt. J. E. Florance; R.S.M., J. J. Cross; R.Q.M.S., H. H. Bevan; Transport, Sgt. R. Fox.

"A" Company.—O.C., Capt. T. G. Gilder; 2nd I/C, Lieut. W. Salvatori; Lieuts. A. Grunsell, T. Norman, J. Hartshorn.

"B" Company.—O.C., Capt. N. S. Cains; 2nd I/C, Capt. A. W. MacDonald; Lieuts. S. R. Nicklin, O. P. Davidson, J. M. Rohan, J. R. Stahle.

"C" Company.—O.C., Capt. H. Percy; 2nd I/C, Lieut. G. Gifford; Lieuts. J. Bruce, S. H. Hubbard, F. T. Hibbard.

"D" Company.—O.C., Capt. E. Beaver; 2nd I/C, Capt. H. C. Bennett; Lieuts. W. H. Richardson, R. C. Blanch, V. C. Stevenson.

Rain commenced to fall when the Battalion moved out on 9th July to Querrieu, where the Companies settled down in shelters and dugouts on the north side of the village, whilst Battalion Headquarters were in the village.

On 11th July Advance Parties left by motor lorry for Vaux and then marched into the Trenches at Sailly Le Sec. The following day the Battalion marched to La Neuville and after resting until dark, marched to Sailly Le Sec and relieved the 46th Battalion. Our Front Line consisted of 14 Posts, which were manned by "B" and "D" Companies. "C" Company was in Support and "A" in Reserve. No Man's Land was thoroughly patrolled during the night, whilst enemy Machine Gun Fire was most active from the series of Strong Posts which he was holding. This resulted in the death of Lieut. V. C. Stevenson, M.M., and several Other Ranks. The enemy was continually shelling Sailly Le Sec and the Back Areas, which gave the Ration Carriers a very rough time.

On 14th the Battalion "B" Team was cancelled and all the men were utilised in the Line, including the Bandsmen. Major H. Wheeler rejoined the Battalion whilst here.

The Front Line Posts were gradually being connected and Dugouts built, but the ground having a bed of chalk and stone, the digging was very strenuous. On 17th the enemy Shelling increased, causing several casualties, including Lieut. J. Bruce, D.C.M., M.M., killed in action, and Capt. H. Percy wounded. On 18th July a Patrol of 1 Officer and 3 men encountered a Party of 12 of the enemy who were establishing a Machine Gun Post in No Man's Land, which was immediately bombed by our men and retired on the run. At 2.30 a.m. the following morning Lieut. S. R. Smith, Scout Officer, and 15 Other Ranks raided two enemy Posts which had been occupied the previous night. However both these Posts were found to be unoccupied. Aerial activity was general over this Sector. An enemy Plane was driven down and the Pilot was seen to descend by parachute and land safely.

On 20th July the Battalion was relieved by the 33rd Battalion and marched to the Reserve Area at Vaire sous Corbie. Whilst here Working Parties were supplied for the digging of new Communication Trenches in the Forward Area and the men also had the opportunity of obtaining baths.

On 24th the 35th Battalion was relieved in the Sector North of Hamel, with "A" and "C" Companies in the Front Line, "D" in Support and "B" in Reserve. Shells were falling fairly heavily on our Support Lines and Cookers, whilst the Ration Carriers were continually being strafed. One of our Planes at night dropped six Bombs on our Sector, apparently by mistake, but no damage resulted.

On 27th July Lieut. W. H. Salvatori walked out into No Man's Land and did not return. Search Parties failed to find him and he was recorded "Missing", apparently a Prisoner of War.

On the night of 29th July Lieut. S. R. Smith with a Patrol attacked an enemy Strong Post and after a sharp fight with Bombs and Rifle Fire, captured one wounded prisoner The following day the enemy Artillery was quiet during the day but at 9.30 p.m. opened up a severe Bombardment on the Front and Support Lines.

On 31st July having been relieved by the 42nd Battalion, the men marched to bivouac at Daours. The weather was wet and the ground muddy. The day was spent in reorganising the Battalion and visiting the Baths.

THE "GREAT PUSH" OF AUGUST, 1918

The Battalion moved on 2nd August to La Neuville, where Lieut.-Col. E. E. Martin, Major F. Grant and Lieut. A. Coolahan, Adjutant, attended a Brigade Conference. Later the Company Commanders attended a Conference on the coming Operation. The next few days were spent in reconnaissance, preparation of Maps and Conferences for the Attack on 8th August. On 6th full details of the operation were received, indicating the Battalion's role as follows:—"C" and "A" Companies to be in support of the 33rd Battalion. "D" and "B" in support of the 35th Battalion. In the event of serious opposition occurring from Accroche Wood, "C" and "D" Companies to move around the North and South fringe of the Wood and then mop up from the Eastern side. On arrival at 1st Objective (Green Line), the Battalion to reorganise a Support Line.

That evening a farewell dinner was given to the Commanding Officer, Lieut.-Col. E. E. Martin, D.S.O., who was leaving the Battalion to return to Australia.

The Company and Platoon Commanders, having made a reconnaisance of the ground of attack in the Accroche Wood Sector and also the route of the Approach March, fully explained the operation to every member of the Battalion, who were in wonderful spirit and confident of success. Lieut.-Col. E. Martin visited all the Companies and addressed the men, wishing them farewell and success and handing over Command to Major F. Grant. The Colonel felt the parting from his men, as there was genuine attachment between them and him, more especially as having passed through trying times with them, he was now leaving when they appeared to be entering the final sphere of operations.

On 7th August the weather cleared and a strong wind dried the ground considerably, much to the relief of all.

That night after the men had been given a special hot meal, the Battalion commenced the march to the Assembly Point, at 10.20 p.m., "A" and "B" Companies taking "A" Track, "C" and "D" taking "C" Track. The Assembly Point was reached and the Battalion was in position by 3.20 a.m. without suffering a casualty. At about 4 a.m. on 8th August a dense fog arose, which made it impossible to see more than a few yards ahead.

When the barrage opened at 4.20 a.m. the men went to the assault with great dash, notwithstanding the great difficulty in keeping direction in the fog and smoke. The tanks, which were to assist in the attack, also had great difficulty in finding their way in the fog.

Very little resistance was offered by the enemy, even in Accroche Wood, and a large number of prisoners were captured. The objective was reached with very light casualties and at 8.20 a.m. the 12th Brigade passed through to commence the second stage of the operation. By 10.15 a.m. the Batallion was on its Objective Line and consolidation was being completed. The cookers were brought up and a hot meal was provided at midday. The total number of prisoners taken by the

Battalion was 7 Officers and 200 Other Ranks. In addition to 21 machine guns and large quantities of stores, many valuable documents were also captured.

As the enemy was now shelling the position, after the meal, the men moved down to old dugouts and shelters in the gully. The next day was spent repairing roads and collecting large quantities of material. Enemy Planes were bombing very heavily but only one casualty resulted. The morning of 10th August broke fine and clear and advance parties were sent to the area held by the 46th Battalion, which was relieved by the Battalion that night, amidst a rain of bombs, but without casualties.

At 3.30 a.m. on 11th August the Battalion was to attack and capture Proyart. This operation was dependant upon the success of a silent operation by the 10th Brigade, timed to commence some hours earlier. At 4.15 a.m. word was received from Brigade cancelling the operation, owing to the failure of the 10th Brigade attack. Fortunately, our Companies had not become involved and were recalled to their former positions. Enemy planes continued their heavy bombing during the night, wounding Lieut. S. Delves and several Other Ranks.

On 12th August the Battalion was relieved by the 12th Manchester Regiment and marched to Vaire sous Corbie. The enemy was busy dropping bombs but the march was accomplished without loss. The weather was fine and hot and the men spent the time resting and swimming in the River Somme. On 14th, information was received that the Battalion would move to the Wiencourt area on the following day and advance parties proceeded to that area. However, Orders were received later cancelling the move. As the enemy planes were now heavily bombing the village, the men were moved out into the fields where shelters were provided.

On 16th August the 49th Battalion in the Liaison Force was relieved on the north of the River Somme. There were numbers of enemy dead still on the Bray-Corbie Road. The march was carried out under heavy shelling and there were some casualties. A London Regiment was on our left and the 131st U.S.A. Regiment on our right.

On 17th the Line was advanced during the night, resulting in Lieut. R. Wight and 7 Other Ranks being wounded. On 19th the enemy kept up a harassing shell fire most of the day, and that night the Scouts carried out a small raid. Identification was required for Brigade information and Lieut. S. R. Smith and his men captured a machine gun, compass and rifle and brought back the required information. During the heavy bombardment Capt. E. Beaver was wounded but remained on duty. On 20th our fighting patrols were very busy over the whole area. The enemy machine gun fire and shelling, however, was very severe. Our casualties were Lieut. V. C. Callen, M.M., and 20 Other Ranks killed in action, and Lieut. G. Barclay and 14 Other Ranks wounded. On 22nd August the Battalion less one Company ("B") became Brigade Reserve to the 35th and 33rd Battalions plus our "B" Company who were to advance the Line. The enemy now commenced to shell our area with guns of every calibre, Battalion Headquarters and the Regimental Aid Post getting their full share as well as the Transport bringing up the ammunition. At 7.0 p.m. the Battalion was ordered to move forward, as the Imperial Troops were reported to be retiring on the left flank, under pressure of an enemy counter attack. The 33rd Battalion, which was holding the Front Line, sent back for further assistance and "C" Company was sent up, the other two Companies remaining in support. In the meantime Capt. N. Cains, O.C. of "B" Company, who had been doing good work by organising a number of the Imperial Troops and reinforcing the left flank, repulsed the counter attack, inflicting very heavy losses on the enemy. Later "C" and "D" Companies made contact with "B" Company. The position at this point was obscure and the men were badly in need of a meal after their strenuous work. At midnight the Ration Limbers arrived at Battalion Headquarters with a hot meal which was sent forward to where the men were holding the line. With Sgt. W. Mudford acting as guide, this was delivered, in spite of heavy shell and machine gun fire, to the men, who had a hot meal whilst actually holding the enemy at bay. The Limbers had a rough trip going back to their quarters through a heavy barrage directed on the roads. Later all objectives were gained and the Companies linked up and formed a Front Line. In the operation 2 Officers and 40 Other Ranks of the enemy were taken prisoner. These were used as stretcher-bearers to assist our own in their heavy work.

Being relieved on 23rd August by 39th Battalion, the Companies marched out independently to a reserve position in the vicinity of Sailly le Sac. A hot meal was waiting for the men on arrival, who rested during the day. Next day Orders were received to move forward the following day, at short notice. Two days were spent standing by awaiting the movement Order. On 27th August the 44th Battalion was relieved in the vicinity of Vaux Wood, where the men were subjected to heavy shell fire and an intense machine gun barrage from the enemy.

The 28th opened with drizzling rain, but it cleared later on. Orders were received to move through the 35th Battalion who were attacking at Curlu. These, however, were later countermanded, as the Imperial Troops on the left flank were failing to keep up with the advance.

On 29th August the Battalion relieved the 35th Battalion in the Front Line and at 5 a.m. pushed out strong Patrols to gain contact with the enemy, from whom slight opposition was met. The 10th London Regiment was still lagging behind in the attack and a defensive left flank had to be established. The Australian Light Horse having reconnoitred the position during the afternoon, another advance was made at 4 p.m. under a light barrage, with slight casualties. This operation resulted in an advance on a front of 1500 yards to a depth of nearly 5000 yards. Again the London Regiment failed to keep up with the advance and defensive flanks had to be established in order to cover the gap. About 30 or 40 of the enemy were killed and 75 prisoners and machine guns captured. At 10 p.m. instructions were received to again attack the enemy position, two objectives being given. The attack was made before dawn, without a barrage. The first objective was reached with few casualties, in spite of heavy machine gun fire. The advance was continued but owing to the intensity of machine gun fire and the fact that the troops on either flank were held up, it was not possible to completely take the objective. The Battalion consolidated its position and on the left flank, owing to the extremely gallant conduct of Lieut. A. J. Grunsell, M.M., who was later killed in action, a strong point was established which played havoc with the enemy in Marriere Wood. At 7 a.m. a request was made for a barrage to assist in the complete capture of the position, but it was decided to postpone the operation until the following morning.

The troops were subjected to intense machine gun fire and severe shelling throughout the day and during the afternoon, about 50 rounds from our own 4.5 Howitzers fell 1500 yards behind our own Front Line. The enemy troops holding this portion of their Line were from their Second Guards Division and the intensity of machine gun fire may be gauged from the fact that when the 33rd Battalion renewed the attack the next morning 100 machine guns were captured on that Sector. During the operation, which gained 1500 yards on a 1000 yards frontage, Capt. A. W. MacDonald, Lieut. A. J. Grunsell and 15 Other Ranks were killed in action, whilst Capt. E. Beaver, Lieut. J. B. Hartshorn and 45 Other Ranks were wounded.

On 31st August, the 33rd Battalion having passed through to the attack, our Battalion was relieved by the 11th Brigade. From 1st to 5th September the men spent resting and going to the baths, and also to a Concert at Suzanne, in spite of active bombing by enemy planes. Whilst here the Battalion was reorganised with 4 Companies and 3 Platoons each and each Platoon having 3 Sections.

On the evening of 5th September the Battalion moved forward in a violent thunderstorm to billet in shelters. The men arrived at their destination thoroughly drenched, but fires were lit and they were soon comfortably settled. Whilst here the Battalion was standing by awaiting orders for a further move forward. Heavy rain set in on the 8th and continued until the 10th. Brigadier-General Goddard inspected the Transport on this day and during the evening the "Blue Gum" Party gave a concert.

On 12th September the Battalion moved up to a position north-west of Halle, where the men were given their packs and blankets and made comfortable. The men were kept busy improving Dugouts, cleaning equipment, training and holding bath parades at Peronne. Enemy planes were very active during the nights dropping bombs. On one occasion two were brought down in flames by one of our night fighters.

On 15th September the Prime Minister of Australia, Mr. W. M. Hughes, attended a Church Parade and gave a short address. Late in the evening of 17th a heavy thunderstorm broke over the area, accompanied by strong wind, which unroofed some of the Dugouts and wrecked the Cookhouse shelters. On 18th the men attended a performance by the 1st Division "Sentimental Blokes", which was highly appreciated by all. During this period cricket and football matches were played near Mt. St. Quentin and also against the 33rd Battalion near Peronne. On 21st a Battalion Sports Programme was carried out and the men generally were having a good time. On 27th September the Battalion paraded in Battle Order and the men were informed of the coming operation, after which they moved to Capron Copse and bivouaced for the night. During the march bombs were frequently dropped along the line, the Transport and Quarter Master's Store receiving special attention at the rear of the column. Whilst proceeding up the gully in the Copse, planes came over flying low and dropped parachute lights over the moving column, enabling them to drop their bombs and use their machine guns freely. The following day the Battalion moved across to Ronssoy Road, where it rested and received orders to move the next day. On the morning of 29th September a move was made to Z Copse, where the Transport and Quarter Master's Store remained. The Battalion moved forward to follow in support of the American Battalions which were to make their first stage of attack on the Hindenburg Line.

After the capture of this by them, our Battalion was to leap frog through them to the Le Catelet Line. The Americans got through the opposition after a hard fight but failed to mop up the area, with the result that our Battalion, following in support, came under very severe machine gun fire in the vicinity of Gillemont Farm, where there were a number of casualties, including the C.O., Lieut.-Col. W. Le Roy Fry. Major F. Grant then assumed command. The Battalion pushed forward and occupied a position on the knoll just behind and to the left of Bony, where the whole situation remained very obscure. During the advance rain fell very heavily, making the going extremely difficult. Our casualties were 27, including Lieut. J. Sneddon who was wounded. On 30th September the Battalion moved to Potts Lane and Duncan Avenue to carry out operations in rear of the 11th Brigade which moved forward at 6 a.m. Headquarters were at Cat Post. Lieut. S. Nicklin with "B" Company joined the 41st Battalion to assist in mopping up in the vicinity of Bony Avenue. This being completed "B" Company remained at Stave Trench. Owing to the rain and intense darkness, difficulty was experienced in getting the rations forward during the advance. They were taken up by pack mules over shell-torn ground with wire lying in all directions, making the track circuitous. The men, however, were given hot meals in the trenches and shell holes which they were holding.

END OF HOSTILITIES

On 1st October the weather cleared and the Battalion moved into reserve at Benjamin Post, with the exception of "B" Company, which was still patrolling Bony Avenue and Stave Trench. During the day a number of H.E. and gas shells came over, but only one casualty resulted.

On 2nd the Battalion moved back to Capron Copse, where it was rejoined by "B" Company and bivouaced for the night. The next day the men marched back to Cat Copse and bivouaced for two days, where the C.O. held an Inspection.

At 1.30 p.m. on 5th the Battalion moved out by light railway and arrived at Peronne at 6 p.m., where hot cocoa and biscuits were served out to the troops by the Y.M.C.A. When leaving Cat Copse four men were wounded by an explosion of cartridges in a fire around which they were standing on the road. At 10 p.m. the same evening the troops entrained for Amiens and arrived there at 6 a.m. on 6th October. Having detrained they marched to billets in Frucourt. The Transport and Quarter Master's Store came by road. The village and billets were comfortable compared with the conditions of recent months.

Whilst here training was carried out in the mornings and sports were held during the afternoons. Lectures on all subjects in connection with the A.I.F. Education Scheme were given. Schools were opened up where men could get experience which would help them in various trades, and occupations on return to civil life. Many went to Farm Schools in the Divisional Area. Organised sports between Companies, Battalions and Brigades were carried out. Debating classes were held and some pleasant and interesting evenings spent.

Soon after settling down, Brigadier-General Goddard inspected the billets and complimented the Transport on their smart appearance. A Battalion Parade was held and the Brigadier spoke of the past eight months' operations on the Somme and of the gallant part the 9th Brigade had played. He urged the men to guard their good name whilst they remained overseas and take it back to Australia.

The weather for the first two weeks was stormy, with the usual amount of mud in evidence, but everything was done for the comfort of the men. Picture shows were provided and concerts were given by Battalion and visiting concert parties, which were greatly appreciated.

Church Parades were held by the Padre, Capt. Chaplain J. Calder. Whilst here Lieut.-Col. A. R. Woolcock, D.S.O., of the 11th Brigade, assumed command of the Battalion. In the course of his remarks during an address to the Officers of the Battalion, he said that in donning the Colours of the 34th Battalion he intended also to absorb the spirit of the Battalion and to continually study the welfare and comfort of the men, which he eventually did in no uncertain manner. Capt. J. E. Florance having left to proceed to Australia, Capt. F. Baulch, the former Quarter Master, rejoined the Battalion to again assume control of the Q.M. Store.

On 11th November, 1918, news was received that Armistice terms had been signed. However, there was very little demonstration on receipt of the news as the men could hardly realise that the War was, for at least some time, actually over.

On 9th December the Battalion marched out of Frucourt to billets at Buigney, which were not very satisfactory and neither was the weather. After a week here a new Billeting Area was found at Miannay and the Battalion moved into this town on 17th December, where the men made themselves quite at home; some enjoying the luxury of comfortable beds. The local people were very friendly, which contributed to a very merry time being spent on the first "Peace" Christmas Day.

Whilst awaiting demobilisation training was very limited. Short Parades being held and Lectures given in connection with the A.I.F. Education Scheme to assist the men on their return to civil life. Books were supplied and classes held covering almost every profession and trade. Quite a number availed themselves of the opportunity of obtaining practical instruction at depots in England and France, whilst a few went to workshops in Belgium.

Sports, football matches and recreation of every kind were carried out and everything possible was done for the comfort of the men. Lieut. F. T. Hibbard had charge of the Educational Lectures. Whilst here, Major H. L. Wheeler left the Battalion for Le Havre and Capts. H. H. Percy, H. T. Hicks and H. C. Bennett, Lieuts. A. G. Farleigh, G. R. Scanlan, R. P. Stevens, P. Flannigan and Blanch rejoined the Battalion.

The first draft for demobolisation, consisting mostly of original members and early reinforcements of the Battalion, left Miannay for Gamaches on 12th March, 1919. After being addressed by the C.O. in the Square, the men moved off for home to the accompaniment of cheers from the remainder of the Battalion, which left on 17th March for Gamaches, where the second draft went into camp on the hill, leaving the balance of the Battalion in the town. The second draft left for Le Havre on 16th April, followed early in May by the final draft.

So ended the War and the 34th Battalion, A.I.F.

BATTLE CASUALTIES

	OFFICERS	OTHER RANKS
Killed in Action	18	343
Died of Wounds	4	105
Wounded	62	1665
	84	2113

BATTLE HONOURS

YPRES, 1917
PASSCHENDALE
AVRE
MONT ST. QUENTIN
FRANCE AND FLANDERS, 1916-1918

MESSINES, 1917
BROODSEINDE
SOMME, 1918
AMIENS
HINDENBURG LINE

OFFICERS WHO SERVED
WITH THE 34th BATTALION, A.I.F.

Lieut.-Col. M. St.J. Lamb
" " E. E. Martin, D.S.O.   (W.) Villers Bretonneux
" " A. R. Woolcock, D.S.O.
" " W. A. LeRoy Fry   (W.) Gillemont Farm
Major C. E. Brodziak   (K.I.A.) Road Wood
" G. R. Clarke (M.O.)   (K.I.A.) Ypres
" W. E. Foxall
" F. G. Grant, D.S.O.
" J. A. McDowell
" H. L. Wheeler   (W.) Villers Bretonneux
Captain W. H. Baker
" F. W. Baulch
" E. Beaver, M.C., M.I.D.   (W.) Clery
" H. C. Bennett
" C. V. Blackett
" B. G. Brodie   (K.I.A.) Warneton
" N. S. Cains, M.C.
" H. N. Dixon
" J. E. Florance
" T. G. Gilder, M.C., M.I.D.   (W.) Ypres
" H. T. Hicks   (W.) Sailly le Sec
" C. S. Jeffries, V.C.   (K.I.A.) Ypres
" A. W. Macdonald   (K.I.A.) Clery
" H. H. McMinn   (P.O.W.) Morlancourt
" R. C. Nowland
" H. H. Percy, M.C.   (W.) Sailly le Sec
" J. W. Richardson   (K.I.A.) Ypres
" R. J. Stewart, M.C.
" C. E. Watson, M.C.
" A. S. Whitlock   (K.I.A.) Messines
" N. H. Bridge (M.O.)
" E. Watson (M.O.)
" J. Calder (Chaplain)
" A. S. McCook (Chaplain)
Lieut. T. Airey   (W.) Le Bizet
" L. J. Avery
" A. Baillie
" G. Barclay   (W.) Bray
" S. W. Barker
" S. W. Bateman
" P. W. Beauchamp
" T. Bellamy   (W.) Villers Bretonneux
" D. F. Berman, D.C.M.
" L. P. Biddulph
" R. Blanch
" P. Bloomfield, C. de G.
" C. J. Bowen   (Died at Sea)
" J. S. Bradbury
" C. S. Brandreth
" E. M. Brissenden
" T. H. Britton, M.C.   (K.I.A.) Villers Bretonneux
" R. S. Brown   (K.I.A.) Morlancourt
" J. Bruce, D.C.M., M.M.   (K.I.A.) Sailly le Sec
" E. Brunker   (W.) Le Touquet
" J. C. Burges   (K.I.A.) Ypres
" S. R. Callaghan   (K.I.A.) Zonnebeke
" V. Callen, M.M.   (K.I.A.) Bray

CORRECTIONS
For Captain N.S.Cains M.C. read
Captain N.S.Cains M.C. & Bar, M.I.D.

For Captain J.Calder (Chaplain) read
Captain J.Calder (Chaplain) M.I.D.

Lieut.	L. G. Clark	
"	P. Coleman	
"	A. E. Collings	(W.) Villers Bretonneux
"	A. F. Coolahan	
"	W. J. Corrie	
"	W. A. Coulson	
"	M. Dann	
"	O. P. Davidson, M.C.	(W.) Ypres
"	O. Davies	(W.)
"	S. H. Delves	(W.) Proyart
"	A. Dowding	(K.I.A.) Villers Bretonneux
"	A. C. Eade	
"	F. East	
"	W. W. Edmonds, M.C.	
"	C. O. Edwards	(W.) Ypres
"	E. C. Edwards	(W.) Ypres
	A. G. Farleigh, M.I.D.	(W.) Villers Bretonneux
"	A. J. Fell, M.C.	(P.O.W.) Morlancourt
"	S. C. Finlay	
"	P. Flannigan	
"	E. Forbes	(W.)
"	F. Furoe	
"	A. J. Gardiner	
"	G. W. Gifford	(W.) Villers Bretonneux
"	D. Granter	
"	F. C. Grimsley	
"	A. J. Grunsell, M.M.	(K.I.A.) Clery
"	C. O. Hamblin	
"	S. M. Harris	(W.) L'Epinette
"	J. B. Hartshorn	(W.) Clery
"	F. A. Hayward	
"	F. T. Hibbard	
"	Hilder	
"	H. S. Hill	
"	G. E. Hodges	(W.) Villers Bretonneux
"	S. H. Hubbard	
"	J. Jackson	
"	A. H. Jenkin	
"	R. T. Kerslake	
"	J. Lang	
"	T. N. Learmont	(W.) Villers Bretonneux
"	F. H. S. Lee	(W.) Villers Bretonneux
"	H. W. Lilja	(W.) Ypres
"	J. A. Longworth	(K.I.A.) Ypres
"	G. Macauley	
"	Macfarlane	(K.I.A.) Villers Bretonneux
"	H. F. Mailer	
"	A. W. Maitland	(W.) Zonnebeke
"	G. Maitland	(W.) Ypres
"	W. W. Matthews	(W.) Messines
"	J. Monfries	(W.) Villers Bretonneux
"	Mulholland	
"	B. G. McKenzie	(K.I.A.) Yyres
"	H. R. McLeod, M.C., M.I.D.	(W.) Messines
"	L. McMahon	(P.O.W.) Morlancourt
"	S. R. Nicklin	
"	T. B. Norman, M.C.	
"	Norris	
"	G. W. Oliver	(W.) Le Touquet
"	H. R. Oliver	
"	J. C. Orr	
"	J. O'Byrne	

Lieut. J. O'Loughlin
 " C. Parkes
 " R. Parkes   (K.I.A.) Villers Bretonneux
 " A. C. Payne, M.M.
 " G. W. H. Perkins
 " E. A. Phillips
 " T. C. Pittaway   (W.) Villers Bretonneux
 " W. C. Purvis   (W.) Ypres
 " E. H. Regan
 " A. E. Rees
 " H. H. Richardson
 " W. H. Richardson   (W.)
 " J. M. Rohan, M.C.
 " W. B. Rothery
 " W. H. Salvatori   (P.O.W.) Sailly le Sec
 " J. B. Sandilands
 " G. R. Scanlan
 " E. Shannon   (K.I.A.) Le Bizet
 " E. G. Sheldon
 " L. T. Smedley
 " J. O. Smith
 " S. R. Smith
 " J. Sneddon   (W.) Gillemont Farm
 " Solomon
 " C. Spencer
 " J. R. Stahle
 " R. P. Stevens
 " V. C. Stevenson, M.M.   (K.I.A.) Sailly le Sec
 " W. Stewart
 " F. D. Thomas   (W.) Villers Bretonneux
 " F. W. Walker   (W.) Messines
 " L. W. R. Warner   (K.I.A.) Messines
 " A. E. Watson   (K.I.A.) Ypres
 " A. L. Watson, M.C.   (W.) Ypres
 " J. Waugh, M.C.   (W.) Le Touquet
 " R. Wight   (W.) Bray
 " T. Williams
 " C. A. Wilson
 " R. Wolstenholme
 " G. T. Wood   (K.I.A.) Houplines
 " A. B. York   (W.) Warneton

ABBREVIATIONS

V.C. — Victoria Cross; D.S.O. — Distinguished Service Order; M.C. — Military Cross; D.C.M. — Distinguished Conduct Medal; M.M. — Military Medal; C. de G. — Croix de Guerre; M.I.D. — Mentioned in Dispatches; K.I.A. — Killed in Action; W. — Wounded; M.O. — Medical Officer; P.O.W. — Prisoner of War.

www.ingramcontent.com/pod-product-compliance
Lightning Source LLC
LaVergne TN
LVHW091320080426
835510LV00007B/581